RELEVANCE OF ADULT EDUCATION

RELEVANCE OF ADULT EDUCATION

OMPRAKASH MANI TRIPATHI

GYAN PUBLISHING HOUSE
NEW DELHI-110002

Relevance of Adult Education

ISBN: 978-81-212-1068-3

Published in 2010 in India by
Gyan Publishing House
23, Main Ansari Road, Darya Ganj,
New Delhi-110002
Phones : 23282060, 23261060
Fax : 011-23285914
E-mail: books@gyanbooks.com
Website: www.gyanbooks.com

Lasser Type Setting by: Rudra Computer Graphics, Delhi
Printed at : Gian Ridhi Offset Printers, Delhi

Dedication

To the memory of my Revered Father Late Pt. Narshingh Tripathi whose scintillating radiance from above instills in me and gives me confidence to carry out the mission of life inherent in service of the youth in Universities and Colleges.

Contents

Foreword 9
Preface 11

1. **Literacy and Adult Education in India** 17
• Meaning of Literacy and Adult Education • Learning Process • The Goal-led Adult Learner • Role of Mother Tongue in Literacy and Adult Education • Literature for Literacy and Adult Education • Training of Instructors • Retention of Literacy Skills • Gains from Literacy and Adult Education • Evaluation of the Literacy and Adult Education Programmes • Historical Perspective on Literacy and Adult Education in India • The Pre-Independence Phase • The 1947-1977 Phase • The Post-1978 Phase • Summary

2. **Socio-economic Context of Eastern Uttar Pradesh** 57
• Socio-economic development • Human development status • Literacy and Adult Education • Summary

3. **NAEP and the TLC in Eastern Uttar Pradesh** 71
• NAEP • TLC • Summary

4. **University Participation in Literacy and Adult Education in India** 81
• Fighting "Exclusion" in Higher Education • University Grants Commission favours

"Inclusion" • Department of Adult, Continuing Education & Extension at Gorakhpur • Summary

5. **Linking Literacy and Adult Education with Development** **117**
• Literacy as an Instrument in Development • Illiteracy and the diversity of Poverty settings • Literacy in Slum settings • Literacy in Rural settings • Economic Development and Literacy • Youth as Pro-Development Change Agents • Summary

Appendices

I. **Tenth Five Year Plan UGC Guidelines on Adult, Continuing Education, Extension and Field Outreach** **147**

II. **Checklists and Interview Schedules Utilized in the Study** **169**
(i) Checklist to assess the relevance of Adult Education Programme
(ii) Checklist for suggestions in regard to the effectiveness of the Programme
(iii) Checklist regarding benefits accruing from Programme
(iv) Checklist regarding benefits accruing from Functionality
(v) Checklist concerning benefits accruing from Literacy
(vi) Interview Schedule for various Functionaries in the Programme

III. **Size of the Programme at the University of Gorakhpur** **177**

Bibliography **179**
Index **201**

Foreword

The Eastern region of Uttar Pradesh has been endowed with the rich natural resource of water; it has also been blessed with a religious heritage that brings people from all over the country, and, from foreign countries including Sri Lanka and Japan. The Handloom industry has also grown remarkably in this part of the country. Another distinctive resource that has attracted national attention in this part of Uttar Pradesh is the network of educational institutions that has grown over the years and the intellectual wealth that it has generated through significant contributions made by individual scholars.

The economic growth of the region has unfortunately not kept pace with the changing times. The industries that flourished in this region (particularly sugarcane) have probably not been able to become the source of major manpower absorption. It has been waiting for the growth of new and appropriate responses to the manpower preferences indicated by the regional, national and global markets. The primary focus of growth in the early part of the twenty-first century has been seen in the emergence and rapid expansion of the Service Industry in such areas as Information Technology, Business Process Outsourcing, Knowledge Process Outsourcing, Information-Technology-enabled Services, Telecommunications, Retail Management, Real Estate Management, Clinical Testing, Medical Transcription, etc.

Alongside, the country has also taken significant strides in social justice areas that call for initiatives towards Universal Literacy, Skills Development Programmes, Self-Help Groups facilitating Micro-credit growth for Micro-enterprise development, Organizations of the Service Providers and Small Producers, Value Addition Processes to Crops available in surplus quantities, etc.

While Universities and Colleges have formulated meaningful responses to knowledge requirements in the social justice areas, it has not been possible to keep pace with the service industry requirements in terms of skills and capabilities. The sector of Adult, Continuing Education and Extension has been visualized by the University Grants Commission as a possible platform within each University to formulate integrated responses to the knowledge and skills requirements of both the social justice sectors and the market-based services industries sectors.

I am happy to find that Dr. O.P.M. Tripathi has worked towards developing a volume that examines the issue of educational needs of the Eastern region of Uttar Pradesh. I hope that the readers would find it a meaningful initiative on his part.

Gorakhpur June 25, 2008

Prof. N. S. Gajbhiye
Vice-Chancellor
Deen Dayal Upadhyaya Gorakhpur University
Gorakhpur

Preface

Literacy and Adult Education in India have substantially meant learning encounters of the adults in formal, informal and non-formal environments. Literacy as a term for Reading, Writing, and handling of Numerals has been seen as a distinct stage in the learning process of the adults largely on account of the sheer magnitude of illiteracy that India faced at the time of Independence in 1947. Literacy as a set of skills has also been seen as an instrumentality that facilitates its own use as a way of life in a written culture environment.

Oracy, or the means of promoting communication through oral means in the form of observing (since body gestures are a part of the communication process), listening and speaking has helped the human society to sustain communication over centuries; the advent of printing systems helped the human race to devise fairly stable ways of storing (and having a record of such knowledge for the succeeding generations) the human knowledge through a set of recognizable characters. Such systems helped the human race to overcome the constraints of distance experienced in the face-to-face interaction.

The modern societies find it convenient to manage systems of Administration, Trade and Commerce, and other forms of interaction through the additional input of literacy. Literacy acquired so much prominence in the formal and informal interactions of the human race that those who relied exclusively on Oracy came to be characterized as Illiterates, thankfully not Uneducated. The advances in Electronics, Communication Sciences, and now Information Technology have, however, made it possible to accord a significant role to the spoken and heard word once again. It has now come to a stage wherein both Oracy and Literacy are beginning to share a significant part of the daily life of an average human being in the modern society. Some believe that Oracy still permeates a large part of his/her daily transactions; others believe that Literacy gives human being a face in the modern society.

Eastern Uttar Pradesh has continued to remain a backward part of the state of Uttar Pradesh, largely on account of lack of Industrialization and the large scale expansion of the Service Industry. This part of the state continues to be dominated by agriculture-based occupations, small handloom factories, and other occupations in the informal and unorganized sector.

Repeated attempts at enhancing literacy rates in the areas have understandably attracted low rates of response; developmental activity in the area has been somewhat slow as compared to other states in the country. Motivation to acquire literacy skills appears to be related to the need for literacy in the lives of the people; life transactions, interactions, or behaviours, if required to be negotiated through literacy skills, would compel people to learn literacy skills. Some may wish away this compulsion by arguing that they could rely on others for negotiating such transactions that require literacy; however, they do realize that it has a social status, a symbolic value that they cannot do without.

I have been a direct witness to the process of slow growth in literacy in the Eastern Uttar Pradesh region. Having been given the opportunity to work in a University Department of Adult, Continuing Education and Extension has given me the additional opportunity of looking at literacy and Adult Education as an organized teaching-learning activity involving issues such as dialect and language, the geographic and socio-economic contexts of the adult persons, the need for learning materials representing a mix of the learner experiences and the rapidly advancing world of knowledge, management systems that help launch Mass Programmes/Campaigns, functionaries that facilitate learning on the part of the people, and Assessment/Evaluation systems that help in the process of certification of learners.

From Literacy Skills to Adult Education, the learners are exposed to opportunities to acquire skills that enable them to negotiate their day-to-day live with a sense of confidence, utilize their skills to manage development in their own lives and help the society to record progress. To many, Adult Education has become the second stage of use of literacy skills for its greater use in life transactions. Some have preferred to call it "Continuing Education" of the learners, particularly when it is believed that the learning process requires a lifelong commitment.

I have made an attempt to analyze the issue of Literacy and Adult Education in the context of Eastern Uttar Pradesh; I have been tempted to look at the larger social issues as an observer of the region and its people. The present book is a sort of look-back on my own life as a person deeply committed to articulating a record of the lives of our fellow-beings.

The book is an expanded version of the doctoral study submitted to the Deen Dayal Upadhyay Gorakhpur University in 1998; the study had sought to document the relevance of and the gains from these initiatives in Literacy and Adult Education. The **relevance** of these programmes was studied in terms of awareness, functionality and gains in literacy. The gains from the programme to the adult learners were recorded as per their own narration. In the process, the learners and the functionaries shared their perceptions on the constraints plaguing the two programmes.

It was a gigantic effort for districts in the Eastern Uttar Pradesh to move towards a state of Total Literacy since some of these had women's literacy as low as 15 percent. The present study takes note of efforts in this regard in Eastern Uttar Pradesh up to 1992 as part of the National Adult Education Programme, and the Total Literacy Campaign launched after the NAEP. It needs to be asserted that the rapid pace of economic development has triggered large scale migration of human resources despite illiteracy; migration to urban areas or towns rapidly moving towards a state of urbanization has generated its own compulsion for the migrants to enhance their awareness levels and skills level to be able to bargain for a better economic deal in the urban areas. Literacy and Adult Education often tend to emerge as the concomitant gains of migration to areas that have higher rates of literacy.

The doctoral study had its limitations insofar it focused on an assessment of the relevance of and gains from the initiatives in literacy and Adult Education within a specified period and based on a small number of Adult Education Centres and Campaign workers. The data for the study was collected through a process involving observation, interview and canvassing the questionnaires. The effect of the Total Literacy Campaign was studied through a process of an Objective Test administered to the learners.

The State is expected to generate better results in the next decade (2001-2011) in view of greater role, responsibilities and powers assigned to the local communities in the management of literacy and other educational programmes as a result of the decentralization initiatives emanating from the 73rd and 74th amendments to the Constitution of India.

I would like to express my sincere thanks to Prof. N.K. Lal, Former Head & Dean, Faculty of Education, D.D.U. Gorakhpur University, Prof. S. N. Tripathi, Head & Dean, Faculty of Education, D.D.U. Gorakhpur University, Prof. Sugan Bhatia, President Indian University Association for Continuing Education, Prof. B.S. Garg, Chancellor, Janardhan Rai Nagar, Rajasthan Vidhyapeeth, Udiaipur, Sri. K.C. Choudhary, President, Indian Adult Education Association, Dr. Madan Singh, General Secretary, Indian Adult Education Association, Prof. Mihir Roychoudhary, Department of Physics, D.D.U. Gorakhpur University, Prof. Manoj Kumar, Department of Fine Arts, D.D.U. Gorakhpur University, Dr. J.P. Dubey, Department of Adult and Continuing Education, Delhi University for their guidance and support. I am deeply thankful to my colleague Dr. Dharm Vrat Tiwari, Project Officer, Dr. A.K. Jaiswal, Project Officer, Dr. (Smt.) Shanti Sharma, Smt. Rita Singh and all the members of the Department of Adult, Continuing and Extension Education, D.D.U. Gorakhpur University for their valuable suggestions in the overall preparation of this book.

I would also like to express sincere thanks to my Mother Smt. Gyatri Tripathi, my wife Smt. Durgawati Tripathi, son Mr. Aditya Mani Tripathi and all other members of my family for their assistance in various ways to make this task pleasant and rewarding.

It would make me feel a little better in my own life if I have been able, through this book, to see life around me with a sense of empathy and understanding.

Om Prakash Mani Tripathi,
M.Sc. (Physics), M.Ed., Ph.D.
Department of Adult, Continuing and Extension Education
Deen Dayal Upadhyay Gorakhpur University
Gorakhpur

June 25, 2008

1

Literacy and Adult Education in India

1.1 Meaning of Literacy and Adult Education

The process of assigning meaning to "literacy" or "Adult Education" has usually been addressed in one of the following three forms:

- Stating a definition,
- Stating the set of needs that it helps to fulfill, and
- Stating the aims and objectives that it seeks to serve for an individual or a society.

The **Census of India** treats a person literate "if she or he can read and write with understanding in any language".

Literacy and Adult Education help adults to learn and to do things in a better way that they will do anyway. Activities of life that are properly negotiated through skills in literacy or through elements of Adult Education are sometimes characterized as base/essential or higher level.

Olson and Torrance (2001) argue that children acquire literacy skills by listening to the literate practices of the parents;

"a literate environment is an important contributing factor. Part of the significance of adult literacy is the important role that adult literates can play in the literate development of their children."

Liveright and Haygood (1969) defined Adult Education as the "process whereby persons who no longer (or did not) attend school on a regular and full-time basis undertake sequential and organized activities with a conscious intention of bringing about changes in information, knowledge, understanding or skills, appreciation and attitudes or for the purpose of identifying and solving personal or community problems."

Adult Education, as compared to Literacy, has been assigned a much wider meaning insofar it includes "in-service, on-the-job, vocational and professional training for different categories of workers and professionals in order to improve their skills; it also enables the adult citizen to acquire necessary aesthetic, cultural and civic education for public enlightenment".

Adults demand education with intrinsic merit, which serves their recognized needs. When an activity helps them solve their problems and makes changes in their behaviour as per their needs, they prefer to participate in such a learning activity. They are at a chronological age where they believe that they are in a position to demand their preferences in learning.

1.2 Learning Process

The primary function of any educational programme is to facilitate desirable changes in the learners through well-designed learning situations. The changes so facilitated can be identified in terms of addition of information and knowledge, in the behaviour of the learners, and ultimately in the attitudes of the learners formed over a period of time. The term "desirable" changes relate to the set of values or purposes that a society cherishes for its members to possess. The learning process is designed in relation to certain pre-articulated or pre-conceived objectives; it is further guided by the selected learning environment in terms of learning materials, learning techniques adopted by the teacher/instructor, and the reward or certification modality envisaged.

The change in behaviour sought to be facilitated by the learning process could be at the level of thinking, feeling or action. "Thinking" represents the intellectual or cognitive aspect of human behaviour; in actual terms, it is the use of ideas or concepts that are identified by the learner to deal with a given problem. "Feeling" belongs to the category of affective behaviours including emotions, and, values. "Acting" or identified actions represents the overt behaviour, the things one actually does or says. The three get integrated insofar what one thinks and what one values has a profound effect on one's actions. Skills in doing things are an important part of actions, and the skills that one uses are affected by one's intellectual preferences, and the values attached to such preferences.

The learning concepts (concepts being basic units by which people think) are tools for thinking, an intellectual framework for problem solving. The following have usually been perceived as concepts critical to adult education:

- **Adults can learn irrespective of their age or state of maturity**. Many adults find sufficient motivation to learn to read and write with a view to reading to their children and encouraging them to read and write.

- **The adult learner has to see both what is going on in reading and why one would invest time and effort in learning**. He does see a meaningful difference between the mechanics of reading and the uses and enjoyment of reading in the hope of making more beginners part of the reading community. "Reading is important to the extent that it connects a reader with his or her own language and culture; if it fails to do this it will often be resisted or ignored."

- **In case of writing, learners need to recognize that "graphic signs" relate to language, not necessarily to meanings or things**. The alphabets are meant to "analyze their speech into discriminable constituents represented by letters and words". Most writing systems represent not meaning directly but the linguistic expression of meaning.

- In adult learning, a classroom or traditional lecture approach is not necessarily the best educational device; learning can take place through other approaches as well. **A meaningful approach to Andragogy would involve a process whereby one makes "written transcriptions of the learner's own spoken utterances with a view to explaining the process of relationship between writing to spoken words**. The learners can then be encouraged to "invent spellings" with a view to questioning their own pronunciation.

- **Adults bring to the learning situation a lot of experience from a wide variety of fields**.

- **Adults, coming into a learning situation, may know more about some aspects of the subject than the teachers or resource persons**. Sometimes, they know more about the entire subject than the teacher or the resource person. This hoids equally true for both well-educated adult participants as well as under-educated adult participants in school or out-of-school.

- While one group of adult learners may have the facilities, the funds or the resources, the other group of adult learners may not, both deserve to be brought actively into the planning process for the learning situation.

Knowles (1970) states four assumptions inherent in the life of adult learner committing himself/herself to any learning process; these are stated below:

1. As a person grows and matures his self-concept moves from one of total dependency (as is the reality of the infant) to one of increasing self-directedness.

2. As an individual matures he accumulates an expanding reservoir of experience that causes him to become an increasingly rich resource of learning, and at the same time, provides him with a broadening base to which to relate new learnings.

3. As an individual matures, his readiness to learn is decreasingly the product of his biological development and academic pressure and is increasingly the product of the developmental tasks required for the performance of his evolving social roles.

4. **Children have been conditioned to have a subject-centred orientation to most learning whereas adults tend to have a problem-centred orientation to learning.**

Critical to the learning process are elements such as *practice* or doing the thing, *reinforcement* or the feedback that ensures that the thing is being done properly, *follow up* or undertaking things in a sequence that follows from the repetition of what has already been done, *satisfaction* about having done the right thing, learning curve or the inevitable taking of time in doing a thing well, and *retention* or the extent to which the new behaviour has been retained by the learner. It has been observed, for example, that people generally remember less than 20 percent of what is shared with them or taught to them. Additionally, concepts are remembered for a much longer period of time than facts.

It could be said, in view of the above critical elements in the learning process, that more efficient learning experiences involve practice, reinforcement and follow up, have a much more lasting effect compared with experiences that focus on remembering a lot of specific facts.

More than 50 years of research in various aspects of Literacy and Adult Education in India indicate a larger number of research studies in the areas of process of adult learning and in development-linked literacy. There appeared to be a preponderance of the goal-led adult learner, functionary training studies, relevance of learning materials studies, learner attitude studies, and, programme impact studies,

1.2.1 The Goal-led Adult Learner

The process of adult learning has been described by a technical term called **Andragogy**; the term is derived from a combination of the classical Greek noun "agoge" (i.e. the activity of leading) with the stem "andr" (i.e. adult). **It is the art and science of leading adult learning, or helping adults to learn**. The term was coined to describe the education theory of the Greek Philosopher Plato. It can be distinguished from **Social Pedagogy** (i.e. basic remedial education for disadvantaged or handicapped adults) referring to Adnragogy as the normal and natural process of continuing education for adults.

Jayagopal (1985) identified the following seven steps that are continuously applied in a circular manner in an andragogic learning situation:

1. Setting a climate for learning,
2. Establishing structures for mutual planning,
3. Assessing interests, needs and values of the adult learners,
4. Formulating objectives for learning,
5. Designing learning activities,
6. Implementing learning activities, and
7. Evaluating results (re-assessing needs, interest and values).

Andragogy could thus be viewed as a learning systems model that uses a feedback loop. It has been considered as a continuous development process for adult learning. The adult learners are responsible for their own development; they must be allowed to set their own purposes. The facilitators in the form of resource persons must view themselves as those available for advice and guidance; they should not view themselves as persons who can determine the scope and sequence of the learning content independent of the preferences articulated by the learners. Often, adult learners want to take from each learning situation only that area of knowledge, skills and attitudes-influencing elements which fit, in their view, their recognized needs.

The adult learners want educational experiences that will help them to negotiate their own life in a more efficient and satisfying manner. They are, for example, not interested in storing away information that they are not likely to use. They want their learning to help solve their actual problems and gain the goals that they have set for themselves. They will not stay long with a text-bound teacher who attempts to make situations and problems fit the pre-determined subject matter. They want to draw upon organized knowledge as a resource that gives more meaning to their experience. They do not want to learn organized knowledge as an avenue to experience.

The adult learners want their learning to be useful in the immediate or near future. They are in the midst of life's pressing problems that demand solutions; any learning with deferred value may hold little appeal for them.

Jayagopal (1985) draws attention to the modified role of the teacher in the adult learning situation in the following words:

"The primary function of the teacher (or facilitator) in an andragogical activity is that of manning or guiding the andragogical process itself, rather than managing the "content" of the learning as in traditional pedagogy. The content of andragogical learning can thus be highly variable, based on the resources and interests of the learners and needs of the institutions and organizations of which they are a part. While the facilitator need not be an "expert" in the learning content, it is more desirable for him to have some "knowledge of content" if he is to guide the "process" effectively.

Unfortunately, literacy initiatives have often been piloted by governments through a process of "centralized control"; these have triggered "a one-way transmission of skills to the masses rather than an occasion for enhancing the competence needed for the empowerment of the individual and community".

Olson and Torrance (2001) have suggested the following considerations to be kept in mind in the planning process of literacy campaigns:

"—. Literacy learning must reflect the specific and diverse contexts of acquisition and use of literacy. These include (1) what the learner already knows, wants and brings to the literacy experience, (2) the mother tongue of the learner, (3) the cultural background of the learners, including family culture, local culture, oral traditions and indigenous knowledge of the learners in relation to gender, class, religion, and race. The process of learning to read is itself an enjoyable and rewarding experience."

The adult learners prefer learning methods that most efficiently develop useful knowledge, skills, habits and attitudes. In short, **adult education is a set of learning experiences that people do for themselves.**

Rashid (1966) sought to measure the level of motivation of a person to acquire literacy skills. He found that the rural areas in and around Delhi were becoming increasingly conscious of the need to have literacy skills; the need to have literacy skills was directly associated with the socio-economic status of the learner. Higher the socio-economic status, greater the desire to acquire literacy skills.

Srivastava (1969) had noted that technological backwardness in tribal areas resulting into low levels of economic development tended to have its effect on the level of interest of the local population in literacy and education; it resulted in a larger drop out rate among the school-going children as well. He further noted that Literacy and Education tended to generate a greater will among the tribal people to access resources made available under the development programmes. Literacy and Education tended to facilitate access to information and knowledge about the various development programmes being operated in their areas.

Chaturvedi 1969) had also noted the positive effects of initiatives in **Social Education** in the districts of Gorakhpur, Jhansi, Lucknow and Mathura; irrigation facilities, for example, facilitated a great deal of change in the methods and pattern of cropping. However, the impact was noticeable more among men, than women.

Dixit (1975) studied the educational need-patterns of the adult learners in urban, rural and tribal communities of Rajasthan. The scholar noted that the learning needs of the adult learners were directly linked to their life problems and occupations including agriculture.

1.2.2 Role of Mother-Tongue in Literacy and Adult Education

The centrality of the adult learners in the learning process raises the question relating to the role of the "mother tongue" in such learning. **Coles (1977)** believes that "mother tongue is the natural vehicle of expression for those who have not learnt to read and write so far in their lives. They have difficulty in developing a full vocabulary in another language or in a national and possibly international language." Learning a vernacular language does not prevent a person later from going on to a national language and provision for this transfer should be accommodated in the scheme of general education.

The arguments in favour of learning only a national or a link language are that it can be used over a wider area, materials can be more economically produced, and, that it is especially useful for town dwellers. It has been further argued by scholars that it promotes national unity. The last argument is a political rather than an educational consideration. There is of course the issue of formalization of syntax, spelling and grammar while initiating plan for development of learning materials for some of the vernacular languages.

All that can be said in regard to the choice of language instruction is that **it is best to teach the learner in his/her mother tongue. UNESCO (1953)** had expressed the same view: that the language of instruction should initially be the mother-tongue of the learner, using the script of the regional/ national language. Then, by a transfer process, the learner should be given instruction in the regional/national language.

The approach held the potential of generating more interest in the learner for the learning situation, make it easier for them to learn, and preserve their pride in their own culture. At the same time, learning the regional language would give them access to the dominant culture and to the larger economic system.

Despite such recognition of the mother-tongue as the medium of instruction, there has been very little systematic research with adult learners on the use of mother-tongue in literacy instruction. Research is certainly available in the area of children learning through the mother-tongue. Those who support the idea of by-passing the mother tongue and teaching only in the second language believe the following:

- The learners become confused by first learning to read in the mother-tongue and then having to transfer to another language.
- Teaching literacy in the dominant language will give the learner tools for admission to the dominant culture and will aid in his or her economic development.
- Some subjects, such as Mathematics, are more easily handled with only one language.
- The learner will learn more quickly and will be competent sooner if all instructions are in the second language.
- The teacher is better trained in the national language than in the local language.

The pro mother-tongue researchers argue with the following points:

- Once a learner has learnt to read, transferring this skill to another language is easy, the second language can be introduced systematically.
- The learner will learn to read more easily if the material makes sense to him or her, and, will be more likely to develop a sense of success in learning, and

- The teacher has a potentially stronger relationship to the community.

Srivastava (1980) undertook to study the effects of using the dialect of the adult learner in the initial stage of a programme in which the final aim was for the learner to acquire functional literacy skills in the standard regional language. The study compares the gains in functional literacy skills when the initial exposure to written text material was in the dialect to the gains when the initial exposure was in the standard regional language, which was not the learner's first language. People taught through the local dialect had no difficulty in learning.

1.2.3 Literature for Literacy and Adult Education

Deshpande (1975) reviewed the Saints literature of the Middle Ages available in the Marathi language; he identified the following learning objectives in the available literature as content for the adult education programme:

- Knowledge of human nature,
- Development of character,
- Motivation to participation in social and cultural development, and
- Recognizing the significance of emotional and national integration.

The writings of the five Marathi Saints – Dhyaneshwar, Namdeo, Eknath, Tukaram, and Ramdas – appeared to have considerable utility as instructional materials relevant to the above stated objectives.

Jacob (1990) identified certain curricular areas in Functional Science and prepared some models for adult education. Through a process of analysis, he found that the Functional Science content areas were neither adequately covered in the Primers for the Adult Education Programme nor were they relevant to the needs of the learners. The learners did not seem to have adequate awareness of the Health Sciences, Home Science, Agricultural Science, and Veterinary Science. He felt that there appeared to be a need for revising the Adult Education Curriculum with more components of Functional Science. He argued that it should be done through a process of needs assessment of and orientations preferred by the adult learners.

Kaur (1992) developed three learning packages for the illiterate adults of Punjab; the package included a Primer dealing with alphabets and matras; the numeracy component dealt with numbers, place, value, simple addition, etc. The Social Science part of the package touched upon various issues of social awareness, and, health and socio-economic problems faced by the local population.

1.2.4 Training of Instructors

Reddy (1990) studied the subject of instructor effectiveness in terms of the socio-psychological factors; it was found that women instructors worked more effectively than men instructors.

Ramadevi (1990) undertook a comparative study of the organization and conduct of various Agencies involved in the Adult Education Programme in Kerala; she noted that the literacy instructors were largely female in the age group of 21-25 years. The Centre for Adult and Continuing Education at the University of Kerala was working better in terms of teaching methods and bringing back the drop-outs. Most instructors had a Master's degree while 14.7 percent had a Ph.D. degree. Learning materials published by the **Centre for Adult and Continuing Education** and **Kerala Association for Non-Formal Education Development (KANFED)** had produced and published learning materials that were used by the other agencies.

1.2.5 Retention of literacy skills

Gadgil (1945) worked towards developing a test of reading and writing by which the lapse into illiteracy could be measured. He noted a positive relationship between the sharp fall in the lapse into illiteracy and the progressive increase of the standard which made a student leave the school. He also noted that it was necessary for a learner to complete a four-year course at school in order to ensure the retention of literacy throughout his later life. The lapse into illiteracy tended to be higher among the middle and lower socio-economic background groups (among the agriculturists and agricultural labourers, and, among the very poor ones).

Khan (1958) found that even with a programme of hundred hours of instruction, the danger of a learner lapsing into illiteracy continued to exist. He found that a 125-hour literacy programme followed by self-education through a library could help contain the incidence of lapse into illiteracy. Retention of literacy skills required continuing access to and perusal of literature in simple language on the topics of adult interest.

Nagappa (1966) noted that the story method of presentation of new ideas had a high appeal for the neo-literates. They wanted to read about topics that had interested them earlier or topics that had a direct link with their occupations. In the rural area, for example, there appeared to be high interest in stories that dealt with the local government, animal husbandry, functioning of village Panchayats, health of the family, and, disease with a larger epidemiological base. He felt that community literacy centres could help enhance the reading interests of the neo-literates.

Mali (1974) studied the factors affecting retention of literacy among the adult neo-literates. He found that the kind of reading materials used happened to be a significant factor affecting retention of the newly acquired literacy skills; Learning materials that had direct relevance to their environment, including occupation, local area problems, etc. drew the adult learners to the learning process

Bhandari (1974) studied factors which affected retention and dropout rates in the adult literacy classes. The dropout phenomenon did not seem to demonstrate any significant difference on account of factors such as age, sex, caste, marital status, occupation, affiliation with economic/social/political groups, schooling during childhood, size of land holdings and adoption of improved agricultural practices. However, such differences surfaced between those who were merely acquiring literacy skills and those who were participants in the functional literacy programmes. **The dropout phenomenon appeared to be more influenced by demands of work relating to farms and animals, pressures of domestic work, ridicule by friends and relatives, distance between home and the literacy centre, etc.** Continuing participation at the adult literacy centre appeared to be influenced by the need to write letters, need to put their signatures on some documents, need to read books on religion, need to maintain farm records and books of accounts, etc.

1.2.6 Gains from Literacy and Adult Education

Kudesia (1973) studied impact of Social Education programme on the social, political, economic, cultural and hygienic conditions of the learners; the study also included changes among the participating learners in terms of self-confidence, self-efficiency, cooperation with others and tolerance towards others. It found that the level of achievement in the health and recreational aspects of development was the highest as compared to other areas in which there was not much change. People remained conservative in respect of caste system, untouchability, poverty and social injustice. Political awareness of the learners also remained at a very low level.

Braham Prakash (1978) undertook a study to assess the gains to the learners from the Farmers' Functional Literacy Programme in terms of their attitudes to and adoption of new behaviours in regard to high yielding varieties, and, attainment in literacy skills. He noted that, leaving aside learners above 35 years, gains were recorded by the actively participating learners in terms of level of knowledge, attitude towards and adoption of the new high yielding varieties, and literacy skills. In functional terms, literate farmers' knowledge about package of practices regarding high yielding varieties programmes was found to be significantly associated with their attitude towards high yielding varieties, but their knowledge was not found to be significantly associated with their adoption behaviour.

Chugani (1987) studied the learning achievement levels in the Rural Functional Literacy Project in North Arcot District in Tamil Nadu; he found that the reading and writing achievement of Class III students were higher than the participants in the Rural Functional Literacy Project. No significant difference was, however, noted in the learning of Arithmetic between the two. Age, caste and family income of the participants were significantly correlated with their literacy achievement.

Sharma (1990) studied role of Literacy and Adult Education in the socio-economic development of the weaker sections in the rural areas of Uttar Pradesh (a case study of rural areas of Allahabad district). He found that the lack of involvement of the development departments in the programme was conspicuous; learning materials were not available, women were not attracted to such classes since their domestic responsibilities prevented them from participating in the activities of the Adult Education Centres.

Bhagria (1992) studied the impact of the centres of Shramik Vidyapeeths on industrial workers and found that the

Shramik Vidyapeeths had played a major role in raising the quality of life, change in the thinking process, and, in the life-patterns of the industrial workers. The learning facilitation process in the area of vocational and technical education had benefited both the workers and the management; wastage in the manufacturing process had gone down considerably. The centres of the Shramik Vidyapeeths also did a good job in areas such Population Education, Civic Responsibility Education, responsible Trade Unionism, and understanding of the Indian Culture.

1.2.7 Evaluation of the Literacy and Adult Education Programmes

Agnihotri (1974) evaluated the adult education programme in the Wardha District of Maharashtra. He found no improvement in their standard of living as a result of the development activities. However, they did assimilate the modern farming methods; many of them understood the necessity of cleanliness. People did, however, continue to be conservative and believers in fate and destiny; they preferred to spend their leisure time praying to God than doing any other work.

Talukdar (1975) surveyed the status of adult education in Assam. He found the management of the adult education programme constrained by several administrative difficulties, shortage of teachers, lack of means of communication, etc.

Murthy (1988) assessed the factors responsible for the effective implementation of the NAEP in Andhra Pradesh. He found that the door-to-door contact by the instructors helped to increase the enrolment; learners favoured the instructors who were regular. In terms of methods of teaching, the learners seemed to like the method that relied discussion-followed-by-demonstration. Content of the programme could have become better with the incorporation of information about business, commerce, marketing, small scale and cottage industries, and, culture. Instructors participating in the programme were likely to be more committed and successful if they had joined the programme for earning a living as compared to those who were mere volunteers not requiring any remuneration or compensation. Mass campaigns did help in creating awareness about the need to acquire literacy skills.

Tantray (1990) undertook an appraisal of the Adult Education Programme in Jammu and Kashmir; he found that location of Adult Education Centres was guided, less by need, more by local pressures. Similarly, instructors were selected from the local community but from amongst respectable families that had some kind of clout with the Project Officers. These instructors were mostly youngsters having studied upto High School and took this work as employment rather than voluntary work. The Adult Education Centres were in the houses of the instructors with little arrangement for lighting, etc. The development departments did not support the work of the Adult Education Centres in any significant manner.

Mohan and Usha (1992) undertook an evaluation of the Total Literacy Campaigns in Bijapur, and Dakshina Kannada districts of Karnataka. The study revealed that there were ideological differences and personal rivalries among the members of the different committees that were hindering the progress even though the organizational set-up was conducive to the programme. The motivational strategies like the Jathas and Street Plays were effective; however, the initial wave of impact gradually waned for lack of sustained enthusiasm on the part of the organizers. Similarly, achievement in the matter of acquisition of literacy skills appeared to be high at levels I and II; however, it tended to go down at level III.

1.3 Historical Perspective on Literacy and Adult Education in India

The historical perspective on literacy and Adult Education needs to be viewed as an important part of the national consciousness. **The great work done by the pioneers of Literacy and Adult Education, both in pre-independent and post-independent India, provides a useful framework for the most recent campaign-based initiatives in this development sector. The historical perspective can be best understood in a two-stage framework: initiatives launched upto 1976-77, and, the phase beginning with the National Adult Education Programme from 1978 onwards. The first phase can be seen as experiments in literacy promotion aimed at specific group of learners; the "post 1978 phase" represents national resolve to utilize every possible resource to attain universal literacy.**

1.3.1 The Pre-Independence Phase

The first trace of governmental concern for Adult Literacy has been noted in the **Report of the Indian Education Commission in 1982**; the **Night Schools** had come into existence with some of these being attached to Mills or Factories or even Jails. The focus in these schools was substantially on Reading and Writing Skills.

The formation of popular government in the provinces in 1937 and the appointment of **The Syed Mahmud Committee on Adult Education in 1938** by the Central Advisory Board of Education revived the governmental concern for Literacy and Adult Education. However, the provincial governments did not last very long to facilitate any substantial spread of Literacy and Adult Education initiatives in the country. In Uttar Pradesh, first the Rural Development Department undertook literacy work with the intent of improving the "moral and material condition of the villagers"; a new Department of

Education Expansion (created in 1938) provided significant leadership to programme. The strategy for the spread of Literacy and Adult Education included adoption of a village each by each of the participating Departments within the government. Support also came from civil society groups like the Ramakrishna Mission, Harijan Sevak Sangh, Labour Welfare Centres, Banks and Factories. Incidentally, this programme supported the celebration of the Literacy Day on July 15, 1939. A Literacy Pledge was signed by some 2,75,000 persons alongside promoting "No Thumb Impression" movement. As part of the movement in Uttar Pradesh, a system of libraries, reading rooms, special books for adults in Hindi and Urdu with focus on History, Geography, Arithmetic and General Science caught up with substantial progress.

The third major initiative in Literacy and Adult Education could be seen in the appointment of a **Liquidation of Illiteracy Committee by the Bombay Congress Committee in 1944-45**; it opened some 70 literacy classes in the city. Many such classes had to be closed down due to disturbances in the city; those left working were taken over by the Bombay City Adult Education Committee in 1945-46. The Mysore State Literacy Council (later rechristened as the Mysore State Adult Education Council) created in 1945 District-level Committees to facilitate organization of literacy classes, follow-up clubs and libraries.

The fourth major initiative has been noticed with the move of the **Imperial Chemical Industries deciding to facilitate all their employees becoming literate through a process of their participation in the literacy classes every day for one hour during their working time without any reduction in their wages**.

1.3.2 The 1947-1977 Phase

In the **post-independent India**, the **Central Advisory Board of Education** appointed, in 1948, a Sub-Committee under the chairmanship of Shri Mohan Lal Saxena to examine the manner in which Literacy and Adult Education could be provided a substantial fillip. Maulana Abdul Kalam Azad, the then Education Minister, termed it as **"Social Education"**, a term that gave it a much broader meaning with focus on education for the complete Man. **Social Education was thus expected to created opportunities for learning that enables human beings to attain harmony with their environment, learn crafts and modes of production for economic advancement, acquire knowledge about elementary hygiene for a healthy life, and, train for informed citizenship.**

The growth of Social Education received considerable attention through the modality of the Five Year Plans; it included setting up of **Social Education Organisers' Training Centres**, the **National Fundamental Education Centre** to train District level officers for Social Education, the **Library Institute in the University of Delhi** to train librarians for the Public Libraries, the **National Book Trust,** and, the **Institute for Workers' Education**.

The **Central Board of Workers' Education** was established to facilitate organization of trade-union supportive education. The **Central Board**, at its level, went on to establish **Regional Workers' Education Centres** in different parts of the country.

The Maharashtra Government worked towards setting up a **Gram Shikshan Muhim in 1959**, probably the first significant initiative in terms of a mass approach to the eradication of illiteracy. The **Mohim** laid emphasis on attainment of "cent-percent literacy" through efforts at the level of each village. This attempted decentralization generated considerable enthusiasm with the village residents vying with each other to achieve "Gram Gaurav", pride for the village. It was claimed that 378 villages in Maharashtra attained complete literacy in the first year itself.

The **Mohim** targeted adults in the age group of 14-50 years; it worked towards reaching out to 20 percent of the adult illiterates each year with a plan in mind that cent-percent literacy would be achieved within a period of five years. The Zila Parishad and the Panchayat Samitis took up leadership of the progamme in right earnest and insisted on a quality of literacy that can be attained, retained and strengthened. The literacy classes were held for a period of three to four months and were aimed at facilitating reading of simple sentences on different topics, learning to count, read and write numbers upto 100, and undertake simple arithmetic operations.

The **Planning Commission** at the level of the Central Government supported the introduction of the Mohim as a pilot project in one Block of each State in the country during the **Fourth five Year Plan**. However, the **Mohim** could not go beyond literacy, lacked infrastructure for post-literacy and follow up work, and, had a very poor financial base.

A Conference of Vice-Chancellors on University Adult Education (Bhopal, July 1966) gave a call for the **establishment of Departments of Adult Education in the Universities** with a view to creating facilities for wider coverage of the illiterate population as also for creating a nation-wide base for technical resource support to the Literacy and Adult Education programmes. The initiative called for a concerted effort to involve students and teachers in the literacy and adult education work with a view to eradicating illiteracy in a period of 10 years. The initiative also called for creation of an environment, in the process of imparting literacy skills that would sustain the use of literacy skills in the lives of the adult neo-literates.

The Planning Commission constituted a **Panel for Literacy Among Industrial Workers in 1964**; it recommended efforts that would make it possible to wipe out illiteracy among the Industrial Workers in the next ten years. At that stage, the resolve entailed spreading literacy among two lakh workers each year; the idea of an age-range for the target group of illiterates in the form of 16-45 years was suggested in the report of the Panel.

The **Fourth Five Year Plan** drew attention to the point of linkage between literacy and socio-economic development; it articulated the view that illiteracy tended to act as a handicap in the process of socio-economic development. The programme of **Farmers' Training and Functional Literacy** was launched in 1968. It drew strength from the belief that a direct correlation existed between physical and human resources and what was critically needed was a linkage between agricultural inputs and the process of upgrading human resources involved in the agricultural operations. Such a linkage, it was felt, could help achieve self-sufficiency in food, and, enhancement in agricultural productivity. The farmers, under this Programme, were trained to acquire new farming practices that ensured higher yield. The components included farmers' training, functional literacy, and, farm broadcasting.

The linkage model of acquiring literacy through participation in development was utilized in many more development sectors – including Elementary Education, Health and Family Planning, Agricultural Extension, Cooperation, etc. Universities and Colleges planned new roles for themselves through involvement of youth enrolled in the National Service Scheme in such programmes.

The **Central Advisory Board of Education** recommended, in its meeting held in November 1974, the introduction of **initiatives in Non-formal Education** through modalities including Multiple-entry programmes, Part-time Education programs, Self-study programmes, etc. The recommendation was converted into various programmes including the **Functional Literacy Programme for the age group 15-35 years, Non-formal Education programme for drop-outs and left-outs in the age group 6-14 years, Correspondence Courses** for those who could not afford to join the regular classes in schools and colleges, and **Satellite Instructional Television** programme for children in primary schools and for adults in the literacy programmes.

1.3.3 The Post-1978 Phase

Jalaluddin (1980) viewed the social significance of the literacy and adult education programmes in developing countries as the most critical factor stimulating thinking about demand creation and meeting the so-created demand through Mass Programmes. He stated the following:

"Launching of massive programmes of literacy and adult education in several developing countries in the recent years is a significant pointer to the growing appreciation of the immediate social significance of these programmes from the point of view of promoting equity and social justice. This brings to focus the need for a new theory and methodology of planning of literacy and adult education programmes. One of the basic demands on such theory would be to underline the different approaches to motivating the adult learners and the literacy workers and educators through creation of demand for literacy, skill learning and continuing education (in contrast to satisfying social demand for formal education) taking advantage of the existing social structures." (p. 3)

The social outcomes of literacy and adult education become critical to the process of planning such programmes; these would drive the various components of programme planning, including the "goal and target-setting exercises, cost-effectiveness in literacy programme planning and management". It is the quality of learning that becomes important in such mass campaigns since the focus is on an assault on the socio-economic constraints experienced by the adult learners. The social change would be reflected in the "power of articulation and expression of the learners as positive social factors".

Such programme planning would hinge upon a strong political will at the national level. **Jalaluddin (1980)** argues the following:

"—. It is the political leadership which can most effectively mobilize and motivate the masses for such programmes. The manifestation of this political will should not only mean enhanced support to literacy and adult education programmes through mass mobilization but also preparedness on the part of national leaders to take hard decisions in the economic and social sectors in favour of the disadvantaged sections of the society."

The **Sixth Five Year Plan** should be seen as a turning point in the national concern for Literacy and Adult Education in India. Literacy and Adult Education attracted a total plan outlay of Rs. 200 crore as against the Rs. 18 crore outlay in the **Fifth Five Year Plan**. Additionally, Agriculture and Rural Development provided separate allocation for the Farmers' Functional Literacy Programme.

The **National Adult Education Programme (NAEP)** was launched on October 2, 1978; it laid down an ambitious target of making literate 100 million adults in the age group 15-35 years within a period of 5 years. The largest-ever target in the history of all Adult Education initiatives undertaken so far was set in the belief that Adult Education would enable learners to play a positive role in bringing about social, economic and cultural changes so that social justice and equity could be achieved. The NAEP had three main components: **literacy**, **awareness**, and, **functionality**.

The **awareness** component was directed towards the emergence of an active citizenry, possessing substantial knowledge about their living conditions, the policies and laws guiding the process of governance and planned development, the rights and duties envisaged for the citizens, and, means that they could employ to enhance their share of participation in the development process. This component of the programme viewed the learner both as an individual and as part of a group of community of learners. Many practitioners stretched it to include **Paulo Freire's concept of conscientization** leading to formation of organizations of the poor in each area.

The **functionality** component brought into sharp focus the skills that the individual learner possessed and should have to negotiate the transaction in his/her daily life with the aim of upgrading his/her conditions of living and in the process contributing to the growth of his family, community, area and state. The rapid migration of citizens from tribal and rural areas to urban areas in search of better livelihood opportunities encountered constraints of living in an urban environment where literacy skills were viewed as significant for awareness about the working conditions and systems of compensation and rights entitlements. Functionality was meant to facilitate improvements in working skills, responsibility in family formation processes, skills in networking for a better and social cohesion, skills in written culture processes as reflected in forms, proforma and applications for accessing basic minimum facilities and other entitlements, etc.

The pre-dominance of purposeful education inherent in the two components of the **NAEP** left its deep mark on the **Literacy** component as well. The entire process of acquiring literacy skills was required to be :

- Relevant to the needs of the learner as experienced in the environment,
- Flexible in terms of duration, time, location and other instructional arrangements,
- Diversified with regard to the curriculum, teaching and learning materials, and teaching methods, and
- Packaged in a sequence and system that was well within the grasp of the learner.

The programme planning authorities were deeply conscious of the need for new management processes suitable to achieving coverage of such a large group of learners. This sensitivity to management was reflected in the attempted consolidation among the existing programmes. The two schemes for the functional literacy among the farmers – the **Kisan Saksharata Yojana** and **Non-formal Education** for the age group 15-25 years were merged and renamed as **Rural Functional Literacy Project** for the age group 15-35 years. The focus appeared to shift from the group of learners to the coverage of learners in a contiguous geographic area. It became possible at this stage to clearly see the shift towards an **Area Development Approach in Literacy and Adult Education**.

The second management sensitivity could be seen in the concerted search for the extremely large number of functionaries required for reaching out to the largest-ever target group of learners. The **University Grants Commission (UGC)** decided to involve Universities and Colleges for the spread of the Adult Education Programme all over the country. The **UGC** planned for a two-phased initiative with the first one going upto March 1985, and, the next one going upto March 1990. It was envisaged that the first phase could promote involvement of all affiliating typing of universities and some 1500 Colleges with the location of some 15,000 to 20,000 Adult Education Centres in different parts of the country. It was further envisaged that the involvement base could be further expanded in the next 5 years with the number of Adult Education Centres going up to about 50,000.

The **Extension** function of the institutions of higher education received significant attention, co-incidentally, around the same period. Under this function, Universities and Colleges were expected to "extend" their physical, technical and manpower resources to tasks that included education of the community in general and the disadvantaged sections of the society in particular in their geographic vicinity. It was believed that if the three types of resources were "extended" to the communities in their vicinity, these resources would bring to the Universities and Colleges insights that could be gainfully incorporated in the curriculum at the Degree and Post-Graduate Degree level courses.

Saldhana, et al (1991) analyzed the work of the institutions of higher education under their third function – Extension; he found that the Extension Programmes had not been integrated with higher education adequately. Such programmes had very little impact on growth in literacy within the areas of their jurisdiction. It was the community-oriented Extension programmes linked to the Undergraduate Curriculum that turned out to be most successful.

The third management sensitivity triggered by the launching of the **NAEP** included reaching out to the out-of-school youth; it was decided to involve the **Nehru Yuvak Kendras (NYKs)**. It should be recalled that the **Chetna Sanghs** organized by the **NYKs** had initiated considerable awareness-generation activity among the rural youth and women.

Thakre (1991) studied the Adult Education Programme launched by the Nagpur University and assessed its impact on the target groups of adult learners. He noted the following:

- Colleges in rural areas participating in the Adult Education Programme responded well in the initial stages; however, the momentum was gradually decreasing largely on account of delayed access to funds for the programme.

- The initial euphoria created for the programme brought in substantial participation by the institutional leaders and the faculty; however, the programme became victim to the usual bureaucratic delays in management at the University and the University Grants Commission levels.

- Bifurcation of the Nagpur University into two Universities – Nagpur University and Amravati University – caused the further decline in the programme.

- Over a period of time, the programme became a mere appendage to the other activities of the Colleges in the rural areas; it did not result into a strong movement at the level of the people in the rural areas.

- The functionaries began to view it as an economic activity bringing in the much-needed remuneration, even though very low as compared to the amount of time spent in teaching-learning processes at the Adult Education Centres and in the communities.

- Scarcity of learning materials created a distance between the learners and the instructors.

In an era where a management shift in literacy and Adult Education could be seen from the learners to the area development approach, girls and women continued to attract special development attention largely in view of the abysmally low rates of literacy among girls and women on the one hand, and, the impact that it made on the family formation processes in the Indian society. **UNICEF** came forward to partner with the Government of India for a special **Non-Formal Education for Girls and Women** in 1982-83; it also led to the establishment of Child Care Centres.

Shramik Vidyapeeths had been conceptualized, on an experimental basis, in 1967 in Bombay with the specific aim of providing integrated education to urban and industrial workers. These institutes had been gradually growing as centres of continuing non-formal education for workers from both the organized and the unorganized sectors of economy. The University/College involvement in the **NAEP** also facilitated the nation-wide spread of the Continuing Education Programme in terms of Short-Term Courses as an alternate channel of non-Dgree-based higher education. Institutions participating in the Adult Education Programme came forward to offer Short-Term Skills-based Courses at the Adult Education Centres with the specific aim of enhancing the functional capacity of the learners from the disadvantaged sections of society.

The **Central Board of Workers' Education** initiated, around this very period, a **Family Adult Literacy Programme for workers** in selected industries, mines and plantations. The **Department of Child Development** launched the **Integrated Child Development Services (ICDS)** programme. The programme now covers the entire country.

In 1983, the educational sector responded to the **New 20-Point Programme** of the then Government by launching a programme aimed at the spread of universal elementary education for the age group 6 to 14 years with special emphasis on girls and simultaneously involve students and voluntary agencies for removal of adult illiteracy. It christened the programme as **Point No. 16**. The programme once again emphasized the following points:

- Planned involvement of Universities/Colleges through students and teachers,
- Promote the process of interaction of universities/colleges with the community so as to accelerate the introduction of Extension,
- Enable the universities/colleges to play a leadership role in a dynamic adult literacy programme,
- Provide special attention towards programmes for women, Scheduled Castes/Scheduled Tribes, handicapped and people from the rural, backward and slum areas,
- Relate the programme directly to the needs, interests, aspirations and life situations of the learners on the one hand and national goals of socio-economic development through a process of operational linkages with the developmental programmes,
- Help in acquisition of basic literacy skills, effective post-literacy, follow up and programmes of continuing education so as to bring the learners in the ambit of lifelong learning processes, and,
- Ensure support to provide adequate infrastructure for administration, resource support, monitoring, evaluation and research for the effective implementation and achievement of goals stated in the Point No. 16 of the new 20-Point Programme.

A Review Committee on Adult Education and other programmes set up by the **UGC** in 1985 suggested the following steps:

- Introduce Extension as the third dimension in all disciplines of study at all levels,

- Develop Adult/Continuing Education Departments/ Centres as separate Inter-Disciplinary Faculty of Non-Formal Education, and

- Launch a **Mass Campaign** by involving the entire student community along with their teachers through special Literacy Camps of 15 days for creating environmental support and awareness among the people.

The same Committee went on to suggest that programmes including Literacy and Adult Education, Population Education, Environmental Education, Legal Literacy, Science for the People, etc. should be implemented at the University level by the Department/Centre for Adult/Continuing Education and Extension.

After a review of the **NAEP** undertaken by the **Planning Commission**, the Government of India slowed down the programme considerably; it was only in 1986 that it launched, what it chose to call, **Mass Programme of Functional Literacy (MPFL)** with a view to eradicating illiteracy from the country as early as possible. By its very designation, the **MPFL** turned out to be literacy functionary-centred programme; it popularized the idea of "Each one, Teach one/ more". An enthusiastic literacy functionary could thus cover up to five to ten illiterates. The **UGC** endorsed the **MPFL** and decided to involve 2 lakh NSS students and 1 lakh non-NSS students of the Universities and Colleges without any monetary incentive or compensation. The **NAEP** had viewed the literacy functionary as someone who required some monetary support or compensation, first Rs. 50/- per month, and, later on rose to Rs. 100/- per month. The Supervisor received a payment of Rs. 600/- per month. There were paid Instructors, Supervisors and Project Officers.

The **Mass Programme of Functional Literacy** continued the **Adult Education Centre** technique of literacy instruction. It also planned for a phased programme of **Post-Literacy and Continuing Education** through what were then called the **Jana Shikshan Nilayams (JSNs)** for a cluster of 4 to 5 villages with a total population of about 5000. The **JSNs** were expected to support the following activities:

- Organize classes for upgradation of literacy and numeracy skills,
- Provide for a library and a reading room,
- Organize **Charcha Mandals** for discussion on common problems facing the community,
- Organize short-duration training programmes on health, family welfare, agriculture, animal husbandry, conservation of energy, improved **chulhas**, etc., and
- Act as a window for securing and transmitting information on development programmes in the area.

It needs to be pointed out that the Post-Literacy programmes did not take off in any significant manner, though a few models were suggested by a **Committee of Experts**.

The prescribed levels of literacy in this programme were the following:

Reading:

- Simple passage on a topic related to the interest of the learners at a speed of 30 words per minute,
- Read with understanding road signs, etc.,
- Ability to follow simple written messages relating to one working and living environments.

Writing:

- Writing at a speed of seven words per minute,

- Taking dictation at a speed of five words per minute,
- Writing with proper spacing and alignment, and
- Writing independently short letters, applications and forms of day-to-day use to the learners.

Numeracy:

- Reading and writing numbers from 1 to 100,
- Doing simple calculations without fraction involving addition, subtraction upto three digits and multiplication and division by two digits, and
- Working knowledge of metric units of weights and measures, currency, distance and area and units of time, and broad idea of proportion and interest (without involving fractions) and their use in working and living conditions.

The programme could not be sustained largely on account of low attendance rates at the Adult Education Centres, participation by children in the age group of 10-14 years along with the adults, poor availability of learning materials and other learning support equipment, inabililty on the part of the learners to be available for a period of eight to ten months for the programme, poor training support for the programme, etc.

The final blow to the programme came in the form of circumstances created by the inequity in compensation levels to the functionaries in the field. Bhatia (1996) detailed the emerging compulsions in terms of the following:

"—. The management resolve to abandon the centre-based approach to literacy acquisition became firm when some of the centre-based functionaries in the literacy programme approached law courts to claim "pay scales" instead of the permissible honoraria. The courts upheld their claims since some of the States had diverted their regular personnel to the literacy programme in order to avoid actual matching contribution to the Central share for the literacy programme."

Next in line of the sequence of several Literacy programmes came in the form of the setting up of the **National Literacy Mission** duly inaugurated by Late Shri Rajiv Gandhi, in May 1988. He appealed to all citizens of the country in general, and the educated persons in particular, to extend their active cooperation by undertaking literacy work as a national service with a missionary spirit. The Government revised the target of covering 80 million illiterates in the age group 15-35 years by 1995.

The Government of India noted the success of the **Total Literacy Campaign** in Ernakulam District in Kerala. The District was able to attain a literacy rate higher than 80 per cent; it was declared fully literate in February 1990. The **TLC** was extended to all the districts in Kerala. It was gradually extended to other districts in the country; Uttar Pradesh had its fair share of the **TLCs** in 1993 in nine districts including Amora, Chamoli, Dehradun (now in Uttranchal), Agra, Ghaziabad, Moradabad, Bijnaur, Bareilly, and Kanpur Dehat.

The **TLC** could be characterized by its following features:

- Area-based, a compact area in the form of a village or cluster of villages, a Nyaya Panchayat or several Nyaya Panchayats, a Community Development Block or several CD Blocks, or a District;
- Time-bound, with the target illiterate population made literate within two years' period;
- Cost-effective, by reducing the cost of making an illiterate person literate at a cost of Rs. 65/- in the plains and Rs. 100/- for hilly and inaccessible areas;

- Result-oriented, the focus being not on enrolment but learning of literacy skills; and
- Volunteer-based, with no provision for salary or honorarium to the volunteer-instructor, but certain provision for respect, honour and appreciation for their service to the nation.

The **Zila Saksharata Samitis (ZSSs)**, created under the **TLC**, laid down their own targets based on surveys conducted at their level, relied on environment building strategies utilizing oral culture and tradition as an effective vehicle of motivating communication, pleaded for literacy and universal enrolment and retention of children in schools, universal immunization, small family norm, women's equality, national integration, etc.

Bhatia (1996) summarized the learning outcomes expected in this programme as "self-reliance in literacy and numeracy, awareness of the causes of deprivation of the poor and the disadvantaged, and action towards amelioration of such conditions through a process of organization and participation in the process of development"

Sachchidananda (1992) undertook an assessment of the Saksharata Muzaffarpur programme, titled SAMU. He found that the school teachers and the students had played a crucial role in the environment building survey, monitoring, and coordination of the SAMU programme. The students had reached out to a large number of Adult Learners themselves.

Rajan (1992) analyzed the working of the **MPFL** in Tamil Nadu; he found that the volunteers were inspired by the Programme as a result of the environment building activities – the rallies, special meetings, guest lectures, special certificates, etc. The learners believed that by participating in the programme, they could read the bus numbers, posters, name boards, and, the newspapers. They could also write letters and applications

Olson and Torrance (2001) raise the issue of the conceptualization of literacy as a possible clue to the success or failure of the literacy campaigns around the world; they state the following view:

"—In many of these programs literacy was seen as a quantitative and undifferentiated phenomenon creating the impression that the problem is of a monolithic nature with a uniform solution. On this understanding illiteracy was seen in terms of deficit or lack in the learner which could be remedied by ready-made packages of knowledge and skill, a marketable commodity with quantitative targets. Such programs have not succeeded as hoped."

The two scholars argue that "literacy must be seen as an activity embedded in social and cultural practice." They provided further explanation in regard to this point:

"—. Literacy and democratic participation become mutually reinforcing, enabling persons and communities to have influence over the factors that affect their lives. When empowering, literacy practices become self-sustaining. Literacy is not something which is delivered, but something to be employed in order to explore their own language and the world on the learner's own terms, which allows them to create and engage in the diverse worlds of literacy."

The failure of some of the literacy campaigns has also been traced to a meaningful understanding of "language, knowledge, and learning needs of the individual and communities involved". Such campaigns have not recognized the "principles of linguistic diversity" while planning literacy programs in local languages". The two scholars refer to a body of research evidence that validates the view that learning to read and write in the mother tongue facilitates both acquisition of literacy but also the learning of a second language.

The historical account of initiatives in literacy and adult education in India offers an insight into "the **shifting perspectives**" to the programme. The shifts effected by the programme planners include the following:

- The adult learner was first perceived as a member of the community in the area with a view to participating in the local development process; he was later seen as an individual who needs to acquire literacy skills for self-interest.

- The intense focus on literacy and numeracy skills in the **NAEP** was followed by a sharp dilution of learning goals in the subsequent phases; the individualized goals tended to share space with the socialized goals.

- The age group characterizing the adult learner has tended to vary within the age range of 10 to 50 years in the different programmes.

- At the level of the objectives of the programmes, a narrowing down appears to have been set in motion through initial attempts at a comprehensive learning initiative to productivity levels of the learners (e.g. farmers, women, and other groups).

- The instructional unit for literacy and adult education changed from an organized learning forum in the form of an Adult Education Centre to an "each one, teach one" situation.

- There appeared to be a distinct shift in the source of ownership or control of the programme; it represented a move from "dominant State control" to a "guided socialization" of programme planning and management processes. The initial Governmental authority changed to the modality of a "registered society" in the form of **Zila Saksharat Samiti**.

1.4 Summary

It would be meaningful at this stage to summarize the insights available from a close perusal of the various literacy and adult education initiatives over a period of more than 50 years in the post-independence period. Some of these lessons learnt have been stated below:

1. Literacy and adult education facilitated at the Adult Education Centres recorded qualitative gains among the learners in terms of greater organized behaviours among them and larger demand for access to social services including elementary education for their children.

2. Learning to read and write with understanding and the use of such skills has been recording slow but meaningful growth. Learner growth, both in terms of literacy skills and Adult Education, continues to be recorded at a fast pace among those how have traditionally lagged behind – women, rural area persons, and persons belonging to the Scheduled Castes and Scheduled Tribes.

3. The coming together of learners at the Adult Education Centres in villages and slum settings helped in the growth of a political consciousness among them; it got reflected in larger percentage of voting at the time of elections.

4. The use of evaluation as a tool to assess achievement or even managerial performance seems to have been undervalued in the process of self-congratulation by the programme managers Districts were declared totally literate without any rigorous evaluation; in some cases,

evaluation teams were sent to the districts after these had been declared as totally literate. The **Dave Committee on Modalities of Total Literacy Declaration and Evaluation of Learning Outcomes** noted the "tendency to inflate their (districts') accomplishment and clamour for having achieved total literacy status". The Committee felt that "unless the learners have acquired retainable and sustainable levels of literacy, the declaration should not be made".

The Campaign approach did well at the level of environment building since the District Collector put all the District's energies for the scheduled period of two months to support the programme; however, there appeared to be a sudden vacuum since volunteers were hard to find. This led many observers of the literacy scene in India to suggest a combination of the two approaches – the TLC approach and the Adult Education Centre approach – with approach-specific functions; it meant environment building through the TLC approach, and, instruction at the Adult Education Centres.

2

Socio-economic Context of Eastern Uttar Pradesh

2.1 Socio-economic development

The resource structure of the State of Uttar Pradesh underwent a significant change with the transfer of 13 districts of the Hill region and the district of Hardwar in November 2000 to the newly created state of Uttaranchal. The State of Uttar Pradesh now covers 240928 sq. kms. with a 7.3 per cent of the total area of the country; the state's share of population is 16.2 percent. It has 70 districts, 300 tehsils and 813 development blocks. It has 52028 Panchayats covering 97134 inhabited villages; it is estimated that a majority of the state's villages are small, with an average population of around 3194 per Panchayat.

The State could be divided into four separate regions – the Western region, the Central region, the Eastern region, and the Southern region.

- **Western region**, comprising of **Agra Circle** (Agra, Aligarh, Etah, Firozabad, Hathras, Mainpuri, and Mathura), the **Barelly Circle** (Bareilly, Budaun, Pilibhit, and Shahjahanpur), the **Meerut Circle** (Baghpat, Bulandshahar, Gautam Buddha Nagar, Ghaziabad, and

Meerut), the **Muradabad Circle** (Bijnor, Jyotiba Phule Nagar, Moradabad, and Rampur, and the Saharanpur Circle (Muzaffarnagar and Saharanpur);

- **Central region**, comprising of the **Kanpur Circle** (Auraiya, Etawah, Farrukhabad, Kannauj, Kanpur Dehat, and Kanpur Nagar), and the Lucknow Circle (Hardoi, Lakhimpur Kheri, Lucknow, Rai Bareli, Sitapur and Unnao);

- **Eastern region** – comprising the **Allahabad Circle** (Allahabad, Fatehpur, Kaushambi and Pratapgarh), the **Azamgarh Circle** (Azamgarh, Ballia and Mau), the **Basti Circle** (Basti, Sant Kabir Nagar and Siddharthnagar), the **Devipatan Circle** (Balrampur, Bahraich, Srawasti and Gonda), the **Faizabad Circle** (Ambedkar Nagar, Barabanki, Faizabad and Sultanpur), the **Gorakhpur Circle** (Deoria, Gorakhpur, Kushinagar and Maharajganj), the **Varanasi Cirlce** (Chandauli, Ghazipur, Jaunpur and Varanasi), and the **Vindhyachal Circle** (Mirzapur, Sant Ravidas Nagar, Bhadohi and Sonbhadra);

- **Southern (Bundelkhand) region** – comprising of the **Chitrakoot Circle** (Banda, Chitrakoot, Hamirpur, and, Mahoba), and, the **Jhansi Circle** (Jalaun, Jhansi and Lalitpur).

Population-wise, the Western and Eastern regions are the most populous with 76.9 per cent of the population residing in these areas. Per capita income in the Western region is almost twice that of the Eastern region.

There appears to be a strong correlation between social inequalities and control over economic assets. Inequalities also exist across gender and social groups. The percentage of population below poverty line has been estimated at 40.8 in 1993-94; this ratio declined to 31.2 per cent in 1999-2000. In addition, the state is characterized by regional variations with some of the districts in Western Uttar Pradesh having higher levels of income as compared to the district in the other regions. Having noted that agriculture is the main occupation in the State, the process of industrialization has unfortunately been concentrated in the Central region and in areas like NOIDA, again close to the Western Uttar Pradesh region.

The State has a population of 16.62 lakhs as per the **Census Survey of India 2001**. It has an adverse sex ratio (898), high fertility and mortality rates (the fertility rate in the state is highest among all states and double that of Kerala), a high proportion of children with children below 7 years constituting 19.03 percent of total population, and, a slow process of demographic change. Urbanization levels are extremely low; the state ranks 14th in the country in this regard.

The **Human Development Report 2003: Uttar Pradesh** states the significance of land in the development process; it points out that "small land holdings continue to be a major obstacle in the development of capital formation and growth in agriculture". It is also one of the main reasons for widespread poverty in the State. This is despite the State being rich in surface and ground water resources facilitating agriculture through tube wells and canal network.

The **Human Development Report 2003** notes that the "economy is dominated by agriculture which engages 66 per cent of its work force". The State is the big producer of wheat, barley, pigeon pea (arhar), potatoes and sugar cane in the country. It is the second largest producer of small millets, rapeseed, mustard, linseed and sweet potatoes.

The diverse religious and social composition of the State's population indicates that Hindus constitute 80.6 per cent of the state's population, Muslims account for 18.5 percent and other religious minorities are estimated to be around 0.9 percent. Among the Hindus, the upper and intermediate castes account for about 22.7 percent of the state's population; the Other Backward Classes constitute 35.5 percent and the Scheduled Castes/Scheduled Tribes number around 24 percent.

2.2 Human development status

The term "human development" refers to strengthening of human capacities including "improved health, knowledge and skills, and participation in civic life" at family, community, area, and the larger societal levels. The **United Nations Development Programme** has been preparing and supporting preparation of **Human Development Reports** based on the following three Indexes:

- Human Development Index
- Human Poverty Index, and
- Gender Development Index.

Human Development Report 2003 of Uttar Pradesh describes the three Indexes in the following words:

"The *Human Development Index* (HDI) is a simple composite measure that measures the overall achievements of a region in terms of three basic dimensions of human development – a long and healthy life, knowledge, as well as a decent standard of living; health status (measured by longevity), knowledge (measured by literacy and enrolments) and a decent standard of living (measured by per capita incomes). These three dimensions are measured by life expectancy at birth, educational attainment (adult literacy and the combined gross primary, secondary and tertiary enrolment ratio) and GDP per capita (PPP US $). Income enters the HDI as a proxy for a decent standard of living and as a surrogate for all human choices not reflected in the other two dimensions.

While the HDI measures overall progress in achieving human development, the *Human Poverty Index (HPI)* measures the distribution of progress through the backlog of deprivation. The broad dimension in which deprivation is measured is the same as in the HDI –health status, knowledge and standard of living.

The *Gender-related development index (GDI)* is the third important index used by the UNDP. It measures the achievements in the same dimensions and uses the same variables as the HDI does, but takes into account inequality in achievement between women and men. The greater the gender disparity in basic human development, the lower a country's GDI compared with its HDI."

Dreze and Sen (1995) have referred to the following five dimensions wherein health and education perform a critical role in the development process:

1. **Intrinsic Importance**: Being educated and healthy are valuable achievements in themselves, and the opportunity to have them can be of direct importance to a person's effective freedom.

2. **Instrumental Personal Roles**: A person's education and health can help him or her to do many things – 'other' than just being educated and healthy – that are also valuable. They can, for instance, be important for getting a job and more generally for making use of economic opportunities. The resulting expansion in incomes and economic means can, in turn, add to a person's freedom to achieve functioning that he or she values.

3. **Instrumental Social Roles**: Greater literacy and basic education can facilitate public discussion of social needs and encourage informed collective demands (e.g. for health care and social security); these in turn can help

expand the facilities that the public enjoys, and contribute to the better utilization of the available services.

4. **Instrumental Process Roles**: The process of schooling can have benefits aside from formal education. For example, the incidence of child labour is intimately connected with non-schooling of children, and the expansion of schooling can reduce the distressing phenomenon of child labour so prevalent in India. Schooling also brings young people in touch with others and thereby broadens their horizons, and this can be particularly important for young girls.

5. **Empowerment and Distributive Roles**: Greater literacy and educational achievements of disadvantaged groups can increase their ability to resist oppression, to organize politically, and to get a fairer deal. The redistributive effects can be important not only between different social groups or households, but also within the family, since there is evidence that better education (particularly female education) contributes to the reduction of gender-based inequalities."

Uttar Pradesh appears to be placed at a low level of human development based on these estimates; it is part of "the lowest cluster of States, along with Bihar, Madhya Pradesh, Rajasthan and Orissa".

The **Human Development Report 2003 of Uttar Pradesh** records the following assessment:

"— the Western region has a marginally higher HDI compared to the Central regions, while the Eastern and the Bundelkhand regions have the lowest HDI."

"— the district with the lowest HDI in UP is Budaun district in Western UP. The other districts (ranked from the lowest) are Baharaich, Sidharthnagar, Hardoi, Maharajganj, Gonda, Shahjahanpur, Sitapur, Rampur and Basti."

The **Report** further points out that "of the twenty districts with the lowest HDI", half of these belong to Eastern UP, five are in Western UP, three in Central UP and two in Bundelkhand. The conclusions drawn in the **Report** indicate a sense of alarm in regard to the status of human development"

- The HDI and GDI are close to the bottom among India's major states.

- None of the UP districts are able to match up to Kerala's performance and only three have an HDI higher than the average achieved in Maharashtra.

- Human poverty is high in UP.

- Despite large differences in income in the UP's districts, levels of human development do not vary as significantly. "Several districts in the Western part of the State have relatively better income levels than the rest but they are among the worst performers in human development or status of women."

2.3 Literacy and Adult Education in the region

The **Census of India 2001** places India's literacy rate at 64.84 percent for the age group of 7 years and above. It treats a person literate "if she or he can read and write with understanding in any language". Male literacy was of the magnitude of 75.26 percent; female literacy was estimated at 53.67 percent. The number of illiterates recorded in that year was 304.11 million; of these 193.48 million were women. The **gender gap in literacy** was placed at 21.59 percent points. The gender gap scenario in literacy becomes grimmer when one looks at the adult population in the age group of 15+ years. The gender gap in this age group amounted to 25.53 percent points.

Apart from the gender gap, the **urban-rural differential in literacy rates** is another critical element in the Indian literacy scenario. The estimates of this differential have been coming down from 1981 (31.20) to 1991 (28.39) and to 2001 (21.18 percent points). The urban literacy rate is in the vicinity of 80 percent; however, literacy rate in the rural areas continues to be below 60 percent. The decline in urban-rural differential has been of the magnitude of 7 percentage points. Literacy rates of females in rural areas are still very low (46.1 percent). The gender gap in literacy rates of urban and rural areas if of the order of 26.8 percentage points.

The third critical factor in the Indian literacy scenario relates to the **literacy status of the Scheduled Castes and the Scheduled Tribes population**. The differential in the literacy rate of the Scheduled Caste population was 14.8 percentage points in 1991; however, it came down to 10.15 percentage points in 2001. Similarly, the literacy rate among the Scheduled Tribes population recorded a low of 47.10 percent in 2001.

A **National Literacy Mission (2007)** document records the following observations in this regard:

"— The corresponding differential in the female literacy rates of the Scheduled Tribes and all communities decreased from 21.10 percentage points in 1991 to 18.91 percentage points in 2001. This differential is still very high and needs special attention if we want to achieve parity in literacy rates of different communities". (2007, p.25.)

The corresponding **literacy rate for Uttar Pradesh** is 56.3 percent. The State has the dubious distinction of having about one-fifth of illiterates in the country. The State had a male literacy rate of 68.82 percent and female literacy rate of 42.22 percent. The hopeful sign in the growth of literacy rate in the State can be seen in the substantial percentage increase in the last decade; literacy percentage grew by 16.7 percent in the last decade as compared to the 13.2 percent growth of literacy at the national level.

The **gender gap in literacy** in the State stood at 26.60 percentage points. The **urban-rural differential in literacy rates** was of the order of 17.22 percentage points. This gap widened to 24.83 percentage points if the **female dimension** was added to the urban-rural differential. The state still ranks 17th among 20 large Indian states, with three-fifth of the women still reported as being illiterate.

Uttar Pradesh is characterized by large gaps between literacy levels in the rural and urban areas; there are also gaps between male and female literacy. It has been observed in the last few decades that **female literacy rates have been rising at a faster rate as compared to the male literacy rate; the net effect is that gender disparity in literacy has been on the decline. However, female-male gaps in literacy are certainly higher than those prevailing at the national level.**

"—while the percentage of female to male literates was 60.8 nationally, this percentage was only 44.8 in Uttar Pradesh. The major gap is in rural literacy where the proportion of female to male literates in just over one-third, compared to more than half nationally."

Disparities in literacy have been observed across social groups as well.

"—The changing pattern of literacy among the social groups shows that literacy among SCs and STs has increased at a higher rate for those groups compared to the general population, but the deficit is sill substantial, particularly among women belonging to these social groups."

The state has the "lowest overall literacy rate as well as female literacy rate in 2001 after Bihar, Jharkhand, and, Jammu and Kashmir". Additionally, **"there are acute disparities between men and women, between social groups, between regions and districts.**" The gender gap in literacy rate is "the third largest", next only to Jharkhand and Rajasthan. It has also been noticed that in the last decade "educationally poor districts have recorded a relatively more rapid rate of improvement, as far as male literacy improvement is concerned but this is not the case with female literacy."

At the District level, the literacy scenario in Eastern Uttar Pradesh varies from 33.82 percent in Shrawasti to 66.12 percent in Varanasi. The male literacy rates vary from 46.47 percent in Shrawasti to 76.18 percent in Jaunpur. The female literacy situation recorded a very grim picture as **Shrawasti had a female literacy rate of 18.58 percent; Varanasi reported female literacy rate of 53.05 percent. Sant Ravidas Nagar (earlier known as Bhadohi) had a gender gap of 37.32 percentage points**. Most districts in Eastern Uttar Pradesh, leaving aside the Varanasi District, reported a male-female literacy differential of more than 25 percentage points.

The **Human Development Report 2003** of Uttar Pradesh undertook a district level analysis of the literacy situation; this analysis indicated "certain important changes" that appear to have taken place in the literacy situation:

"— Between 1981 and 1991, there was a close correlation between the level of literacy of a district in 1981 and the change that it experienced during 1991. In other words, most low literacy districts also experienced low rates of change during 1981-1991. This seems to have changed during 1991-2001. First, the coefficient of variation (measuring the relative distance between districts in terms of literacy), has gone down for total, male and female literacy, but it is still the highest for female literacy."

The **low female literacy-poor performance districts** were the largest in the Eastern region including Bahraich, Mirzapur, Sonbhadra, Balrampur, Gonda, Shravasti and Kushinagar districts. In Eastern Uttar Pradesh, initiatives in literacy in the pre-independence period were virtually non-existent. Some individuals and Non-Governmental Organizations did initiate small efforts. It is only with the advent of the political freedom and independence that significance of literacy to the development process became a major realization.

Attention to the subject of Literacy and Adult Education was drawn from the **Second Five Year Plan** onwards, that too without establishing any separate Department of Adult Education. The Ministry of Education at the level of the Central Government, and, similar Ministries at the State level started planning some programmes. It is only in 1978 that every district in the country was involved in setting up the programme of Literacy and Adult Education; each State Government began to accord the subject a significant status in the process of social development. A Directorate of Literacy and Adult Education has been established under the State Department of Education. Apart from the Government Departments and Agencies, the Universities and Colleges, and, the Non-Governmental Organization were also roped in for a mass national level effort at eradication of illiteracy. All the three agencies utilized the modality of an Adult Education Centre to bring together a group of 30-odd learners in the age group 15-35 years.

The State Resource Centres, created for academic and technical resource support to institutions and programmes related to Adult Literacy, have been allocated to NGOs and Universities in each State. Their functions have been keeping pace with the growth of the literacy and adult education programmes. Their primary task comprises of preparation and publication of basic literacy materials and supplementary learning materials, and training initiatives for the Adult Literacy programmes. These Centres have also established Population and Development Education Units.

The State Resource Centres provide support to the State Literacy Mission as well in the matter of preparing the district plans, training, materials, and monitoring the programmes.

The State Resource Centre for the State of Uttar Pradesh is located in Lucknow. Apart from Primers (it has developed a Primer called "Purvanchal Praveshika" for districts in Eastern Uttar Pradesh). It has additionally prepared Post-literacy materials that include a series of Avadhi Folk Tales (prepared in four parts) for the neo-literates.

Pathak (1991) undertook an assessment of the Adult Education and Socio-Economic Development initiatives in the Azamgarh District"; he noted that the **NAEP** had lost its effectiveness largely due to programme management constraints –e.g. non-supply of learning materials in time, lack of proper publicity, motivation, supervision, lack of sound knowledge of NAEP among the trainers, inadequate infrastructure, lack of departmental coordination, little honorarium, low achievement in functionality and awareness.

The state is expected to generate better results in the next decade (2001-2011) in view of greater role, responsibilities and powers assigned to the local communities in the management of literacy and other educational programmes as a result of the decentralization initiatives emanating from the 73rd and 74th amendments to the Constitution of India.

2.4 Summary

The potential for growth in Eastern Uttar Pradesh can no longer be solely left to better utilization of land resources and water resources. The region needs to utilize its large human resources for the growth the Services Industry. The large network of educational institutions available in the region is likely to be a significant development asset. In addition, the water resources available in the region could generate power that is so essential for the processes of industrialization.

The land resources also hold great potential for generation of jobs provided a process of consolidation of small land holding can facilitate corporatisation of agriculture. The region needs large scale infusion of capital and skills training initiatives for the growth of agro-industries and cottage industries.

The region holds the key of being a major growth centre I view of its proximity to Nepal which is beginning to experience new hopes of growth through democratic processes. Trade between Eastern Uttar Pradesh and Nepal has the potential of growing manifold; this would, in turn, generate demand for both unskilled and skilled manpower.

The fact that the region has 10 districts, of the 20 districts in the State, that are characterized by the lower Human Development Index, calls for a major expansion of infrastructural for health, education, and mass public employment programmes.

There is clearly a need for a massive resource infusion in the form of a Sub-Plan for Women's empowerment in the State, with a larger share of resources for women in Eastern Uttar Pradesh. The low female literacy rates in the region appeared to have an associational relationship with poverty and poor growth performance.

Decentralization appeared to be a critical growth strategy for the region; local level governance processes could generate higher performance levels in both social development and economic development programmes.

3

NAEP and the TLC in Eastern Uttar Pradesh

3.1 National Adult Education Programme

Tripathi (1998) undertook a study of the relevance of the Adult Education Programme in East Uttar Pradesh with special reference to the gains recorded by the neo-literates in the process. The extent of programme was recorded in terms of both the National Adult Education Programme and the **Total Literacy Campaign** in the region. The National Adult Education Programme was launched in a systematic way from 1978 to 1992; the Government of India modified this programme and re-christened it as the **Total Literacy Campaign**. This resulted in the closure of the Adult Education Centres. He viewed the universe of his study in all the Adult Education Centres run by the University and its Colleges and by the Nehru Yuva Kendras.

The sample was selected from among the nine districts – Gorakhpur, Deoria, Basti, Azamgarh, Varanasi, Jaunpur, Gazipur, Balia and Mirzapur – with each District providing two centres in the rural area and two in the urban area. The lottery method provided the mechanism for the selection of the sample. The Centre-level Adult Learners were taken in as sample in their entirety. The sample thus included 36 Adult Education Centres, 419 Male Learners and 519 Female Learners. The Functionaries in the Adult Education Programme were, however, identified as a purposive sample. It was possible to identify 7 Project Officers, 83 Programme Officers, 189 Supervisors, and 914 Instructors.

The sample relating to the **Total Literacy Campaign** was identified in the year 1997-98; it consisted of two Districts – Azamgarh and Mau – that had been able to start the programme from 1992. The Development Blocks running the Total Literacy Campaign were selected for the study. Two villages from each selected Development Block were picked up randomly by lottery method. This exercise provided a sample of 34 villages; learners having completed the **Total Literacy Campaign** accounted for 1342 males and 1516 females.

The researcher used tools such as **Checklists** soliciting opinions of functionaries on issues including relevance and benefits, **Interview Schedule** with the functionaries, and **Achievement Test** for the neo-literates (Appendice – X). The data collection process was undertaken in two phases – in 1991-92 and in 1997-98 with a view to taking a representative sample of work under both the **National Adult Education Programme** and under the Total Literacy Campaign. The Department of Adult, Continuing Education & Extension at the Deen Dayal Upadhyay Gorakhpur University has been implementing the NAEP since 1979-80; the size of the programme has been included in Appendice – XI.

It was a gigantic effort for districts in the Eastern Uttar Pradesh since some of these had women's literacy as low as 15 percent. The low female literacy has been converted into a challenge by some of the districts. **The District of Ballia had, for example, been awarded the Satyen Maitra Memorial**

Literacy Award in the year 2003 for its Post-literacy Programme. The district had a male literacy rate of 71.9 percent and a female literacy rate of 43.3 percent in its rural areas in 2001. The literacy rate in its urban areas had been estimated at 76.9 percent for males and 44.1 percent for females. In comparison to the 1991 Census, the literacy rates in Ballia district increased significantly in 2001; The overall literacy rate registered a 15 percentage point increase. The female literacy rate grew by 17.79 percenage points.

The district launched the Total Literacy Campaign from 1996-2000; it started its Post-literacy Programme in 2001 and completed within a period of one year. It enrolled 2,42,500 learners in the Post-literacy programme and achieved NLM norms among 68.86 percent learners. Among the activity initiatives in the Ballia district, neo-literates were given information concerning the Indira Awas Yojana, Sulabh Shauchalaya, Pension Schemes, Swaran Jayanti Rozgar Yojana, Annapurna and Balika Samridhi Yojana. Self-Help Groups were established by women in 125 clusters. Women who realized the importance of literacy were eager to enroll their children in schools

The present study takes note of efforts in this regard in Eastern Uttar Pradesh up to 1992 as part of the **National Adult Education Programme** and the **Total Literacy Campaign** launched after the **NAEP**; the study seeks to document the relevance of and the gains from these initiatives in Literacy and Adult Education. The **relevance** of these programmes was studies in terms of awareness, functionality and gains in literacy. The gains from the programme to the adult learners were recorded as per their own narration. In the process, the learners and the functionaries shared their perceptions on the constraints plaguing the two programmes.

The study had its limitations insofar it focused on an assessment of the relevance of and gains from the initiatives in literacy and Adult Education within a specified time period and based on a small number of Adult Education Centres and Campaign workers. The data for the study was collected through a process involving observation, interview and canvassing the questionnaires. The effect of the Total Literacy Campaign was studied through a process of an Objective Test administered to the learners.

The respondents were requested to identify any five areas of relevance that they found through their participation in the Adult Education Programme.

Similar **Checklists** were prepared for assessing the areas that required prompt remedial attention with a view to making the Adult Education Programme more effective. The Checklist relating to the benefits perceived by the learners generated some very meaningful perspectives on the people in the region. Some of these have been summarized below:

The responses on the subject of **"relevance" of the National Adult Education Programme** appeared to favour the following items:

- Adult Education Programme will be helpful to eradicate illiteracy from this region: 4.5%

- Adult Education Programme will be helpful developing social, economic, and Political consciousness: 77.75%

- Adult Education Programme will be helpful to put an end to the social ill-traditions Prevalent in this region : 52.42%

The other statements attracted low acceptance.

- The respondents appeared to believe that the **National Adult Education Programme** was an effective scheme for eradication of illiteracy from the Eastern Uttar Pradesh region.

- The Programme was also seen as one that promoted socio-economic and political consciousness among the people in the region.

- It was believed that acquisition of literacy skills spurred curiosity among the people about their socio-economic and political environment. Literate people tended to form their opinions about such concerns based on knowledge gathered from Newspapers, Posters, Banners and Books.

- Heightened consciousness appeared to be a natural consequence of the teaching-learning efforts promoted at the Adult Education Centres.

However, it was doubtful if the phenomenon of social evils could be tackled by acquisition of literacy alone since such practices appeared to have deep roots in the social psyche of the people in the region. Many traditions such as dowry still survive even in well-educated families; literacy could not be the all-pervasive instrument to stamp out such evils from the society.

Other issues – including poverty, population growth, religious tolerance, national integration, growth of a learning society, awareness about governmental development programmes, knowledge about resources available under the various governmental development programmes, etc. appeared to attract low responses.

The respondents appeared to believe that the Adult Education Programme could at best widen the base of literacy in the region; it had also widened knowledge concerning issues facing the region. However, it appeared to be too early to expect changes in social structure, economic or political developments.

In the matter of "benefits" accruing from the Programme, it was noted that the learners coming together at the Adult Education Centres tended to

- Develop a sense of mutual cooperation,
- Gains in awareness concerning health and sanitation, small family norm, savings schemes and government programmes,
- Statements relating to improvements in general knowledge attracted a low score largely because such changes require a considerably large period of time. The activities at the Adult Education Centres tended to concentrate on acquisition of literacy skills.

Gains in **functionality**, insofar these relate to the work environment, were posited mainly in the field of agriculture in view of the predominance of the rural environment. The **Checklist** did contain some statements about various aspects of the small scale industries. The frequency distribution and percentage of responses indicated gains in better management of their occupation, i.e. agriculture, particularly the seeds that result in high crop yields. A large number recognized the gains in the areas of cottage industries including Poultry, Fishery, Piggery, etc.

Did the activities at the Adult Education Centres promote literacy as a way of life? The responses appeared to indicate that the learners were beginning to take the first steps towards participation in a learning society; they were beginning to read Headlines in the Newspapers. There were relatively smaller gains in terms of learning to write and use Mathematics in daily life. An immediate benefit of literacy articulated by the learners related to alertness in saving themselves from the stratagems of cheats and crooks.

Learners and functionaries wanted the environment building component of the Total Literacy Campaign intensified. The learning process could become highly stimulating if its contents were linked with the various economic programmes being implemented in the region. Instructors drawn from Colleges or the University could impart meaningful instruction. They suggested that Village Level Committees should be energized to review the progress of Adult Education activities from time to time. Students working as Instructors would benefit considerably from the inclusion of Adult Education in the Undergraduate Curriculum.

The critical feedback provided by the learners and the functionaries tended to suggest that both the learners and the instructors could be encouraged to meaningfully participate in the programme though a set of incentives or "allurements". The success of such programmes depended on the creation of proper environment.

3.2 Total Literacy Campaign

The **Total Literacy Campaign** was launched in some districts of Eastern Uttar Pradesh in the year 1992-93. The District Magistrate in each district was asked to provide support to and overview the **Campaign** and gear up the entire Governmental and Non-Governmental mechanisms for the **Campaign**. The **TLC** included components such as Environment Building (including *Kala Jathas, Paidal Jathas*, etc.), the teaching-learning process, and, monitoring and evaluation.

A questionnaire containing 17 items on different aspects of the TLC were distributed among the functionaries with a view to assessing the status of the programme on the ground.

During the process of **environment building**, it was found that while the programme had a special target group in mind in the form of learners in the age group of 15-35 years, it became imperative to respond to the learning needs of learners in the age group of 9-14 years since they had also remained deprived of access to educational facilities in the villages. Identification of learners and volunteer-teachers was also undertaken during the environment building phase of the programme.

During the teaching-learning process, several constraints were noted; these included

- shortage of learning materials,
- improper lighting arrangements for the instructional process in the evening hours, and,
- pre-occupation of the learners in work situations.

The functionaries in the programme made the following suggestions to create a better learning environment:

- Supply of kerosene at the place of instruction,
- Timely availability of teaching-learning materials, and
- Provision of remuneration for functionaries.

The overall sense conveyed by the functionaries in the **TLC** tended to suggest that while the Campaign started with a great zeal in most of the selected areas, particularly at the level of environment building, it could not, however, sustain the pace of work due to fault lines in the logistics for the programme. The functionaries, who were primarily from among the Primary School Teachers or the Unemployed Adult Youth, had expected that some benefit would be given to them for participation in the programme; this expectation was not fulfilled.

The **test for reading, writing and arithmetic** capabilities was administered in 17 Blocks and to a total number of 2858 persons. The scores obtained through these tests indicated the following picture:

Marks obtained	*Percentage of learners* *Total*	*Male*	*Female*
Less than 50	9.46	18.28	14.14
50-60	16.77	13.52	15.05
60-70	8.12	19.60	14.21
70-80	19.15	16.95	17.98
80-90	22.21	18.21	20.08
90-100	24.30	13.46	18.54

The **TLC** could be said to be successful insofar it reported fairly high rates of attainment in the three areas – reading, writing and arithmetic capabilities. The attainment levels clearly indicated better results obtained by the female learners.

The researcher advocated the following initiatives to maintain a sustained monitoring of the progress of literacy and adult education in the region:

1. A follow-up study of persons participating in the Adult Education Programme needs to be undertaken with a view to assessing their level of literacy improvement, its effects on their work environment, its effects on their living conditions, etc.

2. A detailed study of the problem, working conditions and psychological support factors essential for the functionaries of the programme should be undertaken through a process of observation and interview; the study should aim at developing best practices for the work environment of the functionaries in the programme.

3.3 Summary

The Chapter reports a research study undertaken by the author relating to the **relevance** of the two literacy and adult education programme initiatives in Eastern Uttar Pradesh; it also analyzed the kind of **benefits** that the learners enrolled in these programmes felt had accrued to them. Both the subjects - of relevance and of benefits - were studied from the perspectives of the learners and the functionaries. These were then cross-checked with the test of achievements of the learners.

In the matter of "benefits" accruing from the Programme, it was noted that the learners coming together at the Adult Education Centres tended to :

- Develop a sense of mutual cooperation,
- Gains in awareness concerning health and sanitation, small family norm, savings schemes and government programmes,
- Statements relating to improvements in general knowledge attracted a low score largely because such changes require a considerably large period of time. The activities at the Adult Education Centres tended to concentrate on acquisition of literacy skills.

Gains in **functionality**, insofar these relate to the work environment, were posited mainly in the field of agriculture in view of the predominance of the rural environment. The responses appeared to indicate that the learners were beginning to take the first steps towards participation in a learning society; they were beginning to read Headlines in the Newspapers. There were, however, relatively smaller gains in terms of learning to write and use Mathematics in daily life. An immediate benefit of literacy articulated by the learners related to alertness in saving themselves from the stratagems of cheats and crooks.

4

University Participation in Literacy and Adult Education in India

4.1 Fighting "Exclusion" in Higher Education

India has more than 300 Universities that produce some 2.5 million graduates each year. Only the US and China produce more graduates than India. There is now worldwide recognition of the significant role that Universities, and more importantly the Colleges that are either constituents of or affiliated to such Universities, have performed in empowering the highly skilled human resources. If parts of the Indian economy are experiencing a boom today, the credit for that goes deservedly to the Universities and the Colleges. This has, of course, been made possible by allocation of substantial resources to education at all stages.

The elementary education system in India has grown into one of the largest in the world. The number of Primary Schools has increased from 2.15 lakh in 1950-51 to more than 7 lakh in 2006-07. Enrolment in Elementary Education has grown nearly six times from 1.92 crore in 1951. This has been further socially deepened by special emphasis on the education of the girl child and that of women. "Education for all" is one such meaningful strategy that India pursues as part of its commitment to "Inclusive" growth. Elementary education is rapidly spreading to villages and tribal clusters with a view to laying the foundations for enhancing the productivity of the work force in these areas. The agricultural sector currently employs 60 percent of the total work force with only 23 percent share of the Gross Domestic Product. The emphasis in the "Sarva Shiksha Abhiyan" will now include quality improvements in Secondary Education – both general and vocational.

Expansion in higher education had met with severe criticism in the last three decades, dubbing our Colleges as "baby-sitting" institutions with the Indian economy unable to absorb much of the manpower trained therein. Indian universities were accused of perpetuating the "mis-match" between the "market and the campus" in regard to the courses that these formulated and offered and the skill demands that the market made. In many cases, our graduates were accused of suffering from "deficiencies in employability". This criticism was sharpest in regard to affiliated Colleges imparting Professional/Technical education in Engineering, Medicine, Software Engineering, Management, etc.

Several observers of the higher education scene in India have made a pointed reference to the poor quality of education imparted by many of these affiliated colleges. The Market has its own ways of applying correctives in case of such graduates; it has devised either on-the-job training for such graduates starting them at lower positions and enabling them to work their way up. Alternatively, many of the graduate from such Colleges have made additional investments in seeking additional knowledge and skills through either new courses or through apprenticeship placement with the Industry either on no payment or one some payment made by the graduates themselves. If the affiliated colleges impart poor quality education, the Market continues to remain a harsh judge of that and expects the graduates to "make up" their deficiencies.

The **National Knowledge Commission**, constituted by the Prime Minister as an advisory body, has noted many constraints in the present structure of the undergraduate colleges. It summarizes the problem in the following words:

"Undergraduate education, which accounts for about 85 percent of the enrolled students, is the largest component of our higher education system. It is imparted through colleges where students enroll for first degrees in Arts, Science or Commerce. There are a total of about 17,700 undergraduate colleges. Of these, a mere 200 colleges are autonomous. The rest, as many as 17,500 colleges, are affiliated to, or constituent in, 131 universities. On average, each university has more than 100 affiliated colleges, but there are some universities each of which has more than 400 affiliated colleges."

The **National Knowledge Commission** believes that one of the ways by which the undergraduate colleges could become more relevant to the higher education needs of their areas is to introduce flexibility in their programme offerings. It suggests the following:

"The first possibility is that some of these affiliated colleges could be remodeled as **community colleges**. *These colleges could provide both vocational education through two-year courses and formal education through three-year courses.* This would serve the needs of a particular segment of the student population better. *They could focus on promoting job-oriented, work-related, skill-based and life-coping education.* These community colleges could provide a unique opportunity to provide holistic education and eligibility for employment to the disadvantaged."

In its recommendations on Vocational Education, the **National Knowledge Commission** has stressed, among others, the following points:

(vi) Vocational training should be made available in various literacy and adult education schemes.

(vii) Schemes for lifelong skill up-gradation, through short training programmes, should be introduced.

(viii) There should be a provision for generating a cadre of multi-skilled persons."

The **NKC** also recommended experimentation with alternate delivery models for such skills training programmes. The following words are quite significant in this context:

"Expand capacity through innovative delivery models: In order to meet the burgeoning requirements of skilled and unskilled labour, a massive increase in quantity of training is needed. The Government may explore new delivery models to increase capacity such as public private partnerships, decentralized delivery, distance learning and computerized vocational training."

The recognition of the principle of "decentralized delivery" of skills training programmes should prompt us to offer the traditional university, over-burdened as it is, as one of the channels through its Department of Adult, Continuing Education and Extension. It has both the channels – its Adult Education Programme, and its Continuing Education Programme – available to it to be able to offer many of what the NKC calls the *job-oriented, work-related, skill-based and life-coping education programmes* without disturbing the undergraduate degree programme structure of three years. In fact, within the three-year Degree programme structure of the undergraduate colleges, a number of such courses can be planned and implemented provided appropriate sub-structures are either recognized or created at the level of the University and the Colleges.

The current boom in the Indian economy has compelled us to revise our earlier assessment of the Indian Universities and the Colleges that are either constituent or affiliated. Investment in higher education in India, particularly in the basic sciences, is finally beginning to generate returns. Kaushik Basu (Times of India, January 30, 2007) argues that while it is important to train computer personnel, fund managers and engineers, investment in more abstract and basic disciplines of higher education – fundamental research, generation of ideas, Pure Mathematics, Theoretical Physics, Literature, Philosophy, and proficiency in English – must not be abandoned. "It is depth in these subjects that helps create a citizenry that is creative and enlightened, and has the ability to absorb technology and innovate".

While it is true that the initial preference of the market for skilled manpower singled out Management Colleges, Engineering Colleges, Financial Management Colleges, etc., the second phase of the economic boom has been looking for manpower in Colleges offering Degree programmes in Arts and Sciences as well. The gap in salaries offered to the Arts and Science graduates may be eight to ten times less than what is being currently offered to graduates of the earlier mentioned Professional Colleges; however, the outsourcing wave of manufacturing and service activities from the Western countries to countries like India and the infusion of industrial capital in small towns and rural areas in the name of real estate development or organized retailing or the spread of financial services has tended to shift bulk of the manpower demand to the Arts and Science Colleges.

The Arts and Science College in India will remain the prime centre for manpower placements in the next

ten to fifteen years. Employers from the market will rush to such Colleges to hire manpower. The critical question however is: Are the Arts and Science Colleges ready for this role? Does the University, of which they are constituent parts or to which they are affiliated, recognize its leadership and mentoring roles in regard to the College youth?

Each University needs to find its moorings in this regard in terms of the evolving priorities in higher education as part of national development. The Prime Minister had highlighted, in his Independence Day Address 2006, the need for a **Vocational Education Mission** in view of the critical need of having a "reservoir of skilled and trained manpower to sustain a high level of economic growth".

Veeraraghavan (1980) had pleaded for "sensitization of the academic community" to the task of rural development. He stated the following three reasons for his perspective in the matter:

"(a) The universities and colleges have the requisite intellectual potential – including research capabilities for analyzing and understanding problems and for identifying solutions.

(b) The idealism and energies of the student youth can be mobilized.

(c) The effects will be long lasting as the quality and relevance of education and learning will itself undergo a change for the better."

However, the university community would need to guard against the "desire to seek personal fortunes", sometimes through short-cuts and questionable means; this would work against the prospect of making "solid contributions to society".

Bhatia (1980) believed, on the other hand, that the university community appeared to be taking a second look at the "nature of relationship between a University/College and its surrounding community". The university community were in the process of examining some of the following questions:

- Should Universities and Colleges remain "insulated from society to pursue knowledge disengaged from its social implications"?
- Should they equip learners with knowledge, skills and attitudes favourable to an effective participation in life – social, economic and cultural?
- Should Universities imbibe knowledge and skills demands made by the market and the society and reflect the same in their curricula?

This inward search has been triggered largely by the structure of the large student body that Universities are responding to each new year. Bhatia (1980) explained the new situation in the following words:

"—. The new student body views education as an instrument for procuring employment, for learning ways to effectively participate in the mechanisms of a secular democratic society. The so-called liberal educational system inherited from the Colonial Powers has not always proved adequate to such aspirations. The critical review of the relevance of higher education started in its initial stages from its unsuitability to the demands of the employment market; it is expanded in its scope by adding such parameters as irrelevance in social, political and cultural terms."

Singh (1980) lamented the fact that despite major endeavors in support of adult literacy and education in the Universities in India in the 1970s, it could not establish itself as "a legitimate programme of activity". He traced the historical perspective on such hesitations on the part of the Universities to accept the programme in the following words:

"—. Towards the end of the Sixties, the **University Grants Commission (UGC)** also began to interest itself in this programme. As a result of its financial and other support several programmes have been mounted but none of them has made any significant impact. Approximately two dozen universities have established Departments of Adult and/or Continuing Education. One University has even embarked upon a Master's programme in Andragogy. Here and there colleges too have been drawn into its activities and the **Indian University Association for Continuing Education (IUACE)** has played some role in stimulating thinking in this direction as well as in initiating certain programmes. The **Ministry of Education** too, operating through the **National Service Scheme (NSS)**, has taken considerable interest particularly in eradicating illiteracy. The agricultural universities, approximately 20 in number, have a somewhat better record of work in so far as each of them has some extension programme. Even here, however, only half a dozen of them have been really successful; the rest have tried but neither sincerely not effectively. All these endeavours do not add up to much. The universities on the whole remain as innocent of extension and adult education work as they were, say, a decade ago."

Singh (1980) traced the slow assimilation of the extension function in higher education to pre-dominant concern of the universities with the "delivery and transmission of knowledge". The Universities tend to prefer delivery of advanced professional education courses in terms of quality that tend to be poor. Singh (1980) passes the following judgement on the quality of advanced professional education in the following words:

"—. But while it would be impossible to quantify, not even one quarter of the activity undertaken by the Indian university performs this professional role with any measure of competence and success. The rest of the universities are engaged in what may be described as 'baby-sitting'. Students do not know what to do when they pass out from School. Their school education prepares them by and large for a white-collar job. Jobs in this sector are scarce. Therefore students partly in order better to prepare themselves for those scarce jobs and partly in the absence of any other alternative, go in for tertiary education. They have neither the inclination to profile from this form of education nor the capacity to do so. And since they constitute the bulk of the student population, it is they who set the tone of work in the universities and colleges. Were they seriously involved in education, it would be a different matter. Most of them are there in order to pass time, to wait till they can get a degree and become eligible for a job in the open market. There is no attempt at learning new skills. No wonder those who are engaged to teach them are neither expected to possess competence of a high caliber nor are they expected to engage them in any serious pursuit of learning. In a sense it is a classic situation of unwilling learners and reluctant teachers, both teaching and learning thus degenerate into a hoax, if one may say so."

He believes that a plan for adult education in Indian Universities is a "plea for relevance, for better productivity, for closer interaction between what is done in the classroom and what is done in the world of work". The university system does not so far place a premium on better productivity. "The moment it becomes aware of the need for putting the focus on better productivity and better learning, an internal shift would take place. The briefest definition of that shift would be that adult education would not be regarded as something additional or marginal but as something centrally integral to the process of education."

India witnessed a period of socio-cultural disadvantage wherein the entire formal system of education tended to represent the preserve of vested interests representing the upper middle class; such groups were also labeled as "elitist social structures" that tended to influence development planning processes to serve their interests. Formal education, right from the school stage to the College/University stage was planned to suit their backgrounds, preferred hours of the day, and classroom language suited to their class of people.

The recognition that upper middle class groups could no longer continue to be the sole determinants of the development planning process ushered in a period of socio-economic development planning for the poor with a view to creating opportunities for them to upgrade their current level of education and employment. The **National Adult Education Programme** was, probably, the first mass attempt at enabling the poor and the illiterate to acquire literacy and numeracy skills; it was expected that the adult illiterates so influenced by this Programme would begin to push their children for enrolment in the Primary Schools. The functionaries for the Programme were drawn from among those who had or were in the process of gaining from participation in formal education at school, college or university levels.

The **NAEP** thus represented the first mass movement to usher in a culture of "Inclusion" in the sphere of education. An ambitious plan was drawn up to upgrade the illiterates' level through literacy, Adult Education, Non-formal Education, and Vocational Skills Training.

The **National Adult Education Programme,** the **Point No. 16 of the 20-Point Programme**, and other Literacy Campaigns as part of the work of the **National Literacy Mission** has certainly helped alter the illiteracy profile of the country. The gains in removal of or reduction in the percentage of the illiterate population have had their share of influence on the number of those enrolling for elementary education. These gains have substantially been due to the gains in reduction of illiteracy among the female population. The programme planners of literacy and adult education have also refined their perceptions on what motivates illiterate persons to acquire literacy. The changing perceptions of the planners' led them to introduce **Functional Literacy** for diverse groups of population (prominent among them being Farmers and Women).

The second most important factor that has contributed to substantial reduction in the size of the group of illiterates is the growth of the Service Industry that values manual labour with basic literacy skills. This Industry values basic literacy skills in such jobs as Construction, Loading, Retailing, Handlooms, Bidi-making, and several other micro-enterprises. The growth of jobs in the Service Industry created an impetus for Migration to diverse geographic centres of employment opportunity; the entrepreneurial instinct that supported migration necessitated acquisition of literacy and numeracy skills since people so venturing out was responding to the inherent fear of moving to unknown places.

The nation-wide literacy and adult education programmes required a very large number of literacy and adult education functionaries who could facilitate the acquisition of literacy and numeracy skills. Next to the large community of Primary School Teachers in India (who get drafted for every kind of mass initiative of the Governance processes), students in Schools, Colleges and Universities offered themselves as the largest ever group of functionaries that could support a nation-wide programme. The 1978 **National Adult Education Programme** thus identified three groups of literacy functionaries from within the Government, Schools/Colleges/ Universities, and, Voluntary Agencies. The out-of-school youth were sought both by the Voluntary Agencies and prorgrammes of the Central Government like the **Nehru Yuva Kendra Sangthan**.

University/College participation in the Literacy and Adult Education Programmes brought in not just the students as volunteer-instructors, but the teachers as well. Alongside promoting social mobilization in the community through interaction with opinion leaders and family elders, the teachers began to raise serious questions concerning the purpose of organizing Adult Education Centres on the one hand and the motivational orientations of the learners coming to such Centres.

Bhatia (1982) raised the following issues in this regard:

"If the adult education classes are merely restricted to the three R's and creating an awareness of the various community problems, these may fail to sustain the interest of the adults. They should cover both the components of formal knowledge as well as the prominent needs of their environment. The rewards should also correspond with those available from the system of formal education.

The greatest challenge lies in analyzing the environmental peculiarities of each community and applying those insights to preparation of teaching and learning materials and instructional strategies. Concepts governing the details of the teaching content must emerge from the features of the community environment, dominant occupations, geographical and ecological conditions. This would require intensive and properly motivated pilot research programmes handled by experts who are both knowledgeable and sympathetic. Unfortunately, we do not have models of evaluative or analytical designs which could be utilized in adult literacy programmes; research in non-formal education has not received much attention in our country."

The University-based scholars pointed out, for example, the critical choice of the "local language" for the Literacy and Adult Education programme. The issue involved extensive research into areas such as the nature of verbal repertoire, the range and function of speech, the socio-linguistic domains, etc. The situation tended to become further complex where both the "standard language" and the "local dialect" had distinct domains of use. The instructional context relied upon the standard language for formal classroom interaction and textbook preparation; the oral interaction both in and outside the classroom registered the pervasiveness of the local dialect. The learners felt a since of "disconnect" with the teacher by virtue of the model of language that he/she tended to rely upon. The textbook guided the volunteer-teachers to ignore the validity of the local dialect as a vehicle of communication; they tended to foster virtual contempt towards the dialect.

4.2 University Grants Commission favours "Inclusion"

The **Conference of Vice-Chancellors** held in 1977 at Rajkot, Gujarat, mooted the idea of Universities launching a nationwide programme of outreach to the communities areas within their jurisdiction

The first set of **Guidelines issues by the UGC**, way back in 1979, stipulated the following rationale for such participation:

"1.2 In order to discharge the responsibility to the education system and to the society as a whole, the university must assume adult education and extension as an important responsibility and give it the same status as teaching and research. These should be made an integral part of the objectives and functions of the University/College.

1.3 It is important to establish an organic link between adult education/extension and University curricula. The former should not be looked upon merely as a welfare activity for the deprived social groups, but as a means for making higher education relevant to the needs of the society and oriented towards a solution of existing problems. Without such interaction on a continuing basis, the Universities will remain isolated from the society and their programmes out of tune with the reality around them."

Bhatia (1980) viewed the Guidelines issued by the UGC as specific pointers for a University-based and University-led outreach process; it took the following concrete forms:

"More attention is now being paid to the idea of a university going to the community, extending its resources in the service of the weaker section of society and to others who have remained outside its area of operation. When a university or a college goes to the community, it takes with it a group of people and set of services for a certain period of time. It goes to the community with two specific objectives in mind:

- To broaden the socio-cultural perspectives of students and teachers through an exposure to conditions of living and areas of knowledge which may not otherwise be available to them within their experiential range; and

- To bring about specific changes in the locality through provision of service and imparting of information, skills and change in attitudes of the target population in the community."

Universities and Colleges had accorded Extension the same status as in case of Teaching and Research way back in 1977. The **Policy Frame on Development of Higher Education (1977)** provided the framework for Extension of physical and technocratic resources available with the institutions of higher education to dissemination of knowledge and skills in the community, with special preference to disadvantaged sections of the society.

The UGC reiterated the emphasis in 1983 and 1985 by UGC. It asserted that the University system has a responsibility to the society as a whole. All universities and colleges should develop close relationship with and support with the local communities, and all students and teachers must be involved in such programmes as an integral part of their education. The **National Service Scheme (NSS)** programme should be expanded and improved. It should be the obligation of the teaching community to give extension lectures to interpret recent trends in their domains of knowledge and how it applies to the process of solution of problems faced by the community. Universities can also help in the preparation of development projects for the communities around them, including the rural community. Such involvement will also help in bringing relevance into the courses at the under graduate and the postgraduate level and into the research programme".

The National Adult Education Programme provided the UGC an opportunity to operationalize the idea. **Bhatia (1996)** described the enabling factors for such a move:

"—. Youth in universities and colleges provided the volunteer manpower required for a large scale nationwide programme; academic and technocratic resources available in these institutions were also considered for technical resource support to the programme in addition to the support being provided by the Directorate of Adult Education at the national level and the State Resource Centre at the State level. The areas of technical resource support included curriculum development, preparation of teaching-learning materials, training, post-literacy and follow-up materials, monitoring, evaluation, research and innovation."

This programme was operationalized by the UGC on the basis of a Project approach with the help of a self-contained and accountable organizational unit; a period of five years was considered adequate for imparting literacy skills to the entire adult population in the age group of 15-35 years numbering about 100 million adult illiterates. The learning outcomes were seen in terms of **literacy** (reading, writing and numeracy), **functionality** (improvement of the skills of learners to cope with challenges of daily living), and awareness (getting to know the causes and sources of one's deprivation, improvement in work skills, better control of the work and socio-political environment, and, knowledge about policies and programmes launched for their right to development.

The University Grants Commission, in its document titled – **Consolidating the Past, Strengthening the Future** (2004) – has traced the historical perspective of the involvement of institutions of higher education in the programme of Literacy and Adult Education in the following terms:

"UGC acknowledges the leading role played by universities and colleges in bringing about social change through outreach activities. UGC has been using adult and continuing education as an effective tool for lifelong learning and outreach activities under its Non-Formal Education programmes.

The scheme was initiated in 1971 to promote elementary education amongst illiterates and Neo-literates of the weaker sections of the society. UGC assists University Centres / Departments of Adult Education by pursuing various adult and continuing education programmes by involving the teachers and students. These programmes, among others, focus on literacy, post-literacy, continuing education, science for people, environment education, legal literacy and technology transfer. At present there are 79 adult and continuing education centres / departments in the country. Six new centres have been set up during 2004-05."

Universities and Colleges, through their teachers and students, have been nurturing a kind of social sensitivity that reminds these privileged segments of society to facilitate upward mobility for those often characterized as the "disadvantaged sections" of society through literacy, education and training. These institutions have, in a way, paid their respects to the generations of social reformers who have been reaching out to millions of illiterates through mass education programmes centred on the need to attain freedom from foreign rule and give substantive socio-economic content to self-rule.

4.3 Department of Adult, Continuing and Extension Education at Deen Dayal Upadhyay University Gorakhpur

The Union Finance Minister reminded the nation, while presenting his Budget for the year 2007-08, that the "declared objective" of the Eleventh Five Year Plan is "Faster and More Inclusive Growth". Among the other objectives of the Eleventh Five Year Plan are:

- Growth of 4 percent in the agricultural sector,
- Faster employment creation,
- Reducing disparities across regions, and
- Ensuring access to basic physical infrastructure as well as health and education services to all.

There is a strong case for every University in the country, and the Colleges as well, to find a great deal of relevance in these objectives for their own agenda. Like the nation, each University has to evolve strategies that would enable it and its Colleges to create an enabling environment for the youth on their campuses and those in the surrounding communities towards making speedy progress towards attainment of these objectives.

This would, however, imply a serious reconsideration of the focus or the mandate that the Departments of Adult,

Continuing Education & Extension decide for themselves. Should the focus continue to be on Knowledge Dissemination of the well-codified and documented knowledge in the field of Adult and Continuing Education, or, in the larger field of Extension?

Many universities have opted for this focus by attaching high priority to Teaching Programmes at the Post-graduate Diploma or MA or Ph.D. programme levels. This has been chosen despite the recognition of the paucity of well-codified and documented knowledge from within the national context. Apparently, this had either been chosen on account of the push from within the University for offering teaching courses at the post-graduate level, as is the case with other knowledge-based Faculties and Departments. The caveat accepted by most universities in such situations lay in the recognition of the need to generate knowledge from the dynamic lives of the adult learners located in tribal clusters, rural and urban areas. There is a need to undertake an assessment of how much of such knowledge generation within the national context has taken place in the last nearly 30 years of growth of the Departments of Adult, Continuing Education and Extension in our universities.

Some Universities chose, through their Departments of Adult, Continuing Education and Extension, to concentrate their energies in the adoption of areas and communities through a process of identifying the educational needs of the people therein and planning and implementation of programmes that enabled them to seek knowledge and skills sufficient enough to participate in the area development process with dignity. The educational needs so identified brought recognition within each University that what the area or community people required multiple knowledge resources available across Faculties and Departments. Such roles made the staff in the Departments of Adult, Continuing Education and Extension emerge as "knowledge managers" and "knowledge generators", rather than pre-dominantly "knowledge disseminators" and occasional "knowledge generators". This whole question of job designation led to an identity crisis since the University knew well Professors, Readers and Lecturer and found it extremely difficult to come out of its age-long slumber to recognize designation of new roles with equality in service and other work conditions.

There need not be necessarily any "identity crisis" provided the University Administration recognizes its commitment to national development goals and programme priorities articulated in that behalf. It is a question of recognizing legitimate constituencies for knowledge dissemination, knowledge generation and skills training. The constituency need not be restricted only to the enrolled students in its various teaching programmes; the constituency must be seen in terms of areas and communities within each University's jurisdiction in terms of their knowledge need to overcome development constraints.

A University usually devotes itself to the tasks of knowledge dissemination (of the available codified and documented knowledge), skills training, and knowledge generation through research that provides a better understanding of the lives of the people in the community. The village, the tribal cluster and the urban settlements must be its laboratory to generate knowledge, apart, of course, from the advancements made in the laboratories. It is essential then that the three tasks must be well-grounded in the adopted village, tribal cluster or urban settlements within the vicinity of each institution.

It must raise questions as to whether the present growth patterns are "Inclusive" and "faster". If not, what

are the constraints that obstruct such a process on the ground. Are its graduates and post-graduates "employable"? Does it have a profile of its surrounding geographic entities and the state of human resources in such geographic entities? Are the youth low on employability for deficiencies within its own ways of functioning? Or, are these structural constraints that are rooted in the resource structure of the surrounding geographic entities and the state of human resources therein? Is it doing enough to provide both to its youth and to the larger community both the soft skills of inter-personal communication and negotiation and the hard vocational skills that the market attaches priority to?

Each University needs to consider if it would be appropriate to institute or locate a structure that would respond to the geographic entity- or community-based demands for knowledge dissemination, skills training and knowledge generation tasks. Can it consider the existing Department of Adult, Continuing Education and Extension as a Hub for these tasks to generate a consultative and implementation process for responding to the "employability needs" of youth within campuses and those in the larger communities that it adopts.

A central Hub for these tasks should ordinarily lead the consultative process on the subject of each university and college "adopting" a surrounding geographic entity for knowledge dissemination, skills training and knowledge generation. It should develop an inventory of "skills in demand" in the form of a bank for subsequent use for developing courses and programmes on each of the skill areas. It should identify a resource persons' pool that can support the process of training in the skill areas; such a pool of resource persons should, of course, be identified both from within the campuses and those

actively working in the trade and industry. It should utilize the technical competence available with such resource persons to generate learning materials and problem profiles for use in the instructional process in the courses. It should utilize the services of the pedagogues to determine if such course materials can be made amenable to self-learning with guidance available on reference.

Each University and College should think in terms of creating adequate infrastructure to facilitate "placement growth" for their students. This should include the following:

- **Setting up a Placement Cell,**
- **Website for Campus Placement,**
- **Linkages with the Alumni now with Industry,**
- **Forging relationships with firms/companies/ industries,**
- **Start courses for soft skills including personality development, negotiating interviews and resume writing, Modules on literacy, numeracy, communication skills, entrepreneurship and other general skills relevant to workplace requirements, and**
- **Screen students on the basis of case studies, sound academic record, and, communication skills.**

If examples are needed to support the above view point, the **Indira Gandhi National Open University (IGNOU)** has recently decided to be the finishing school for the unemployed educated. **IGNOU** would also

- Identify the types of knowledge and skilled work force required for regional, national and global development,

- Classify knowledge and skills available with graduates coming out of Colleges,

- Identify gaps in the existing skills of College graduates in relation to the skills required by the market, and

- Provide instructional support for additional knowledge and skills.

The process of adoption of a village, a tribal cluster and an urban settlement should necessarily entail preparation of resource profiles of these geographic entities. In case of villages and tribal clusters, for example, the most critical problem that would be commonly experienced would relate to ways and means of enhancing agricultural productivity. It been attempted by introducing high yielding varieties, improved methods of farming, and introduction of agro-processing industries; it is now sought to be strengthened by attempting to enable surplus labour in agriculture to industry by imparting work skills that industry requires. The **Special Economic Zones (SEZs)** are being canvassed to infuse large scale industrial capital in rural areas. The initiative has met with very good response in some states like Gujarat, Maharashtra, Tamil Nadu, Andhra Pradesh, Haryana and Punjab; however, it has encountered popular resistance in a state like West Bengal.

The **SEZ** rush has suddenly taken people by surprise in most of the states. There is need to generate and disseminate knowledge about the gains and constraints in industrialization of rural land; there is also need to impart skills to the landowners and the landless labour in these areas to comprehend the consequence of such a move on their livelihoods and the skills that they require in seeking a just and honourable compensation including rehabilitation rights. Must they be forced to sell their land? Or, are their ways by which they are invited to contribute their land to an SEZ with the ownership rights to land still intact and a partnership in the industrial activity? These are soft skills, but are very critical to the right to survival with dignity of the people. There are some hard skills as well that need to be canvassed.

The **Union Budget for 2007-08** accorded a priority status, for example, to the following skills in demand:

- Self-employment initiatives sought to be promoted through the **Swaranjayanti Gram Swarozgar Yojana (SGSY)** among the rural poor through Self-Help Groups (skill area: **formation and management of Self-Help Groups, Micro-Insurance**),

- Self-employment initiatives sought to be promoted through the **Swaranjayanti Shahari Rozgar Yojana (SSRY)** – (skill area: **micro-enterprise management, Micro-Insurance**),

- Coaching support to recipients of **Post-Matric Scholarships for students belonging to the Scheduled Castes, the Scheduled Tribes, and the Socially and Educationally Backward Clusters** (skill area: **soft skills in communication**, and, **coaching support in subject areas like Mathematics, Sciences and Social Sciences**),

- Coaching support to recipients of **Post-Matric Scholarships for students belonging to Minority Communities** (skill area: **soft skills in communication**, and, **coaching support in subject areas like Mathematics, Sciences and Social Sciences**),

- Growth of micro-credit programmes through formation of self-help groups and their linkage with financing institutions like **NABARD, SIDBI** and other Banks (skill area: **formation and management of self-help groups**; knowledge generation area: **review of The Micro-Financial Sector (Development & Regulation) Bill, Financial Inclusion Fund, and, Financial Inclusion Technology Fund),**

- E-Governance for rural and urban areas (skill area: **participation in governance skills, transparency and accountability enforcement skills**, etc.)

The rapid growth of the services sector in the Indian economy has opened up a number of new possibilities in terms of manpower needs. The College youth appear to be eminently suited to competing for such positions provided the Centralized Hub in the University works towards development of the following short-term courses:

- Insurance services and their management,
- Reverse mortgage scheme for senior citizens,
- Financial Services Planning and Management including Mutual Fund Product Investment Promotion,
- Organized Retailing,
- Micro-franchising in Telecom Business,
- Beauty Culture and Cosmetology,
- Fashion Industry,
- Travel and tourism management,
- Airline Ticketing,
- Airline Hospitality Management,
- Software Engineering,
- Animation Graphics,
- Business Process Outsourcing and Call Centre industry,
- Training to be a Radio Jockey,
- Training to be a Disc Jockey,
- Real Estate Development,

A large number of new and emerging knowledge areas are gaining widespread notice; it should be possible for the

Centralized Hub in the University to train some young persons in these areas for possible placement with national and international NGOs and other institutions. These include the following:

- Self-Help Groups for Micro-Credit,
- Micro-insurance,
- Micro-enterprise Development and Management,
- Soft skills in communication,
- Participation in governance skills, including transparency and accountability skills
- Insurance services and their management,
- Reverse mortgage scheme for senior citizens,
- Financial Services Planning and Management including Mutual Fund Product Investment Promotion,
- Organized Retailing,
- Micro-franchising in Telecom Business,
- Beauty Culture and Cosmetology,
- Fashion Industry,
- Travel and tourism management,
- Airline Hospitality Management,
- Software Engineering,
- Animation Graphics,
- Training to be a Radio Jockey,
- Real Estate Development,
- Climate change,
- Satyagraha as a form of social and political protest,
- NGO Management,
- Disaster Management,
- Right to Information Advocacy,
- Public Interest Litigation

The number of short-term skill-based courses continues to grow with Universities and Colleges forming partnerships with the active players in the Industry and other private providers of training services. The next few pages either summarize the developments in a particular skill area or list advertisements that market players have been utilizing to attract youth for such courses.

The next logical step lies, of course, in collecting more such content and re-framing it in the form of Course Titles, Objectives, Content, Instructional Methodology, Instructional duration and its sequencing, learning assessment processes, and, certification processes. Based on such details, the organizing institutions needs to work out a fee structure for each course.

The **Grameen Bank** in Bangladesh, under the stewardship of Mohmmad Yunus, has pioneered poor people's access to credit for capital and other requirements for their micro-enterprises. It is believed that such Groups have so far given loans amounting to $5.72 million in the process generating profits amounting to some $15 million. The number of clients that such Groups have reached out to in terms of facilitating access to credit numbers some 8 million persons. And most of them are women.

Studies have pointed out that women accessing credit from these institutions have followed the two-child norm; it is believed that their "independence and empowerment" emanated from success in running micro-enterprises in their areas with profit. **SEWA Bank** (managed by the Self-Employed Women's Association in Ahmedabad) has made it possible for their poor women members to use credit productively as part of their concern for the sustenance needs of their families. The **Working Women's Forum** in the southern states and the **Annapurna Mahila Mandal** in Maharashtra provide both credit and social support services including educational, medical, legal assistance, and enterprise training.

In the business world, the poor are increasingly being seen as "bankable". The practice has been growing in India since the last three decades. The earlier backdrop of local moneylenders charging exorbitant rates of interest (varying from 40% to 75%) finds fairly tough competition from such **Self-Help Groups** that offer small loans to their members out of the poor of resources saved by them.

Many Public Sector Banks and Private Sector Banks are beginning to take increasing interest in reaching out to the Self-Help Groups both under the priority lending initiatives announced by the Government of India and in the belief that these are profit-making operations. The HDFC Bank's experience indicates that the recovery of low cost housing loans has been an incredible 100 percent.

The **Reserve Bank of India** estimates that the total micro-credit demand in India is estimated around Rs. 1,50,000 crore; the actual disbursement have not so far gone beyond Rs. 8,000 crore. The average loan amount per person is around Rs. 4,000. An assessment of the number of Self-Help Groups indicates that 60 percent of such Groups are concentrated in Andhra Pradesh, Tamil Nadu and Karnataka. The purposes of seeking loans have tended to vary from "subsistence creation" to "livelihood creation" and "livelihood finance".

The lending capacity of the Self-Help Groups to provide credit to their members is being augmented through **National Bank for Agriculture and Rural Development's Bank Linkage Programme**. The programme has connected many SHG's with formal banks. Philanthropic organizations like the **Ford Foundation, the Bill and Melinda Gates Foundation** and **ACCION International** have provided considerable assistance to the SHG activities in the form of grants. A **World Bank study** has highlighted the need to improving governance and promoting internal transparency with greater participation on the part of the members.

The **International Labour Organization** has been supporting training programmes whereby Self-Help Groups could exploit the strong synergies between micro-insurance and micro-credit for the sheer safety of assets created under the micro-finance programmes.

The entry point for manpower in the **Call Centre industry** usually tends to veer round a Degree with fluency in English language speech and comprehension. A number of private institutions have been offering courses to train personnel for this job. Included among such institutions are the Bharathidasan University at Tiruchirappalli; the University is offering the course at various locations including Delhi. In its initial stages, the industry mainly looked for voice-based customer support; however, the industry now expects diversified services having a direct effect on the enhancement of revenues and profits of the companies that outsource work to India. BPO units are now expected to undertake analysis and take decisions both relevant and beneficial to the client's business context.

The Industry itself offers what it calls "soft" training sessions and induction exercises as part of its efforts to "acclimatize fresh employees". The increase in functionalities required, need is being increasingly felt for injecting elements of specialization in such training processes. Investor or consumer contact with the goods and service providers has been creating needs for such domain specializations; such operations are now being instituted by those setting up the organized retail trade, financial services, technology hardware and software, hospitality industry, legal services, research and development, etc.

As initiatives in training and development grow, one can notice the formulation of customized training programmes. These programmes encourage self-learning, interactive web-based training sessions, company intranet-based training sessions, personality development and technical courses, short-term workshops, and hands-on projects on client sites in foreign locations.

Communication training includes voice and accent training, subject domain training, skill and attitudinal training. Youth working in supervisory positions require training in coaching, mentoring, stress management, handling called moods with patience and politeness, etc.

Nagarajan, founder and COO, 24/7 Customer, in an interview to the Times of India, March 7, 2007, listed the following expectations from his employees:

- Good command over the English language, and
- Sound analytical skills and the urge to the extra mile to exceed client expectations.

Others expect knowledge management, data security, team management skills, knowledge of and fluency in foreign languages like French, Spanish, Mandarin, Japanese, Italian, etc.

As part of the **Policy Frame of Development of Higher Education** formulated by the **University Grants Commission**, several State Governments in India encouraged the Universities within their jurisdiction to evolve forms for institutionalizing the Extension function in higher education. Universities located in the backward regions of the State of Uttar Pradesh readily came forward to assimilate such ideas and established appropriate structures aimed at harnessing teachers and students in the task of eradication of illiteracy and provision of knowledge-based and skills-training-based educational initiatives.

The **Department of Adult, Continuing and Extension Education at Deen Dayal Upadhyay Gorakhpur University** was established by the University in April 1979 as part of the its efforts to operationalize Extension as the third dimension of higher education in India. It established Remote Community Centres to offer education in the community through students and teachers in the University and its Colleges. It added the Continuing Education Programme in 1982 through the modality of Short-Term Courses for those learners in and outside the University and its College who were keen to upgrade their knowledge and skills. It established Population Education Clubs in the University and its Colleges in the year 1984-85 to make learners and other youth aware of the critical relationships between Population size and the right to access development opportunities. It started Jan Shikshan Nilayams (JSNs) in 1988 for neo-literates graduating from the Education Centres; the JSNs offered facilities for Post-literacy and Continuing Education activities at the Panchayat level in the project areas of the University.

The Department of Adult, Continuing and Extension Education has been working towards formulating and offering a number of non-Degree-based Short-Term Courses to youth within and outside the campus of the Deen Dayal Upadhyaya University in Gorakhpur. Youth within the campus sought such courses apparently with a view to find a place for themselves in the employment market, or, with a view to enhancing study skills that brought within their knowledge multiple sources of information and knowledge. Youth outside the campus, and equally important constituents for the Department, sought such courses as a result of their initial participation in the Adult Education Programme located in various areas in the city.

Most such courses continue to be skill-based, skills that either brings the youth closer to the employability demands of the market or skills that seem to work as "finishing touches" to their school or college education. Girls and women from the community participating, for example, in the Fashion Designing course offered by the Department appeared to have varied motivations. While some find it a meaningful resource to set themselves up in the Fashion Trade as an economic activity, others find such skills equally in demand within their own household at the one level and bringing in a new perspective on their own choice of fashion. Those who participate in the Software Engineering courses offered by the Department find themselves providing services like data entry, data management, and data storage to clients in the market; some of them find their internet-based study skills adding to the resource called knowledge so critically required in higher education.

The Department had organized a National Seminar in 2007 to identify ways by which this process could be expanded in scale through the participation of colleges affiliated to the Deen Dayal Upadhyaya Gorakhpur University. It had been suggested that the Department of Adult, Continuing & Extension Education should work towards placing itself as the **Knowledge dissemination, Knowledge generation, and Skills training Hub** in regard to employability demands made by the Market, including Trade and Industry.

Such a centralized Hub located in the University could evolve a set of functions that are supportive of the emergency of the Degree College as a similar Hub within its own area of jurisdiction at the level of each District. Colleagues in the Department have been working towards evolving a vision for such structures at the level of the University and its affiliated Colleges.

The programme managers within the Department continue to remain alive to the challenges that lie ahead and would like to re-dedicate themselves to the processes of networking with resources and institutions that are so vital to the sustenance of such initiatives. Since 1992, the Department of Adult, Continuing and Extension Education at the Deen Dayal Upadhyay Gorakhpur University has been offering Continuing Education Programmes both through a process of financial support from the University Grants Commission and on a Self-financing basis.

The Department's work at the community level comprises of the following activities:

- Environment building, Survey, and Training programmes for the functionaries,
- Post-literacy and Follow Up activities for the Neo-literates,
- Short-term Continuing Education Course for weaker sections of the society,
- Continuing Education activities – including setting up Libraries, organization of Post-literacy classes, information window, cultural activities, sports and games, etc, and
- Population Education activities.

At the University level, the Department organizes the following activities:

Courses under Equivalency Programme:

- Computer applications,
- PC Assembling, Maintenance and Repair,
- Unix & C,
- Desktop Publishing,
- SMPS and Monitor Repairing, and
- Computer-aided Financial Accounting.

Certificate/Diploma/Advanced Diploma Courses under quality of life improvement:

- Fashion Designing,
- Beautification,
- Computer-aided Graphics and Fashion Designing, and
- Spoken English.

Courses under Vocational/Career-oriented Programme:

- Visual Arts,
- Cookery and Ice-Cream Making,
- Bakery and Confectionary,
- Photography,
- Still and Motion Photograph, and
- Interior Decoration.

The above-stated courses are offered on a self-financing basis. A total number of 4292 students have participated in these courses.

The Department also conducts Short-term Continuing Education Courses for low-income groups; these include courses in Fruit Preservation, Making Socially Useful Products (envelope-making, Bindi-making, etc.), Tailoring, Sewing Machine repairing, Baking & Confectionary, Health, Nutrition and First Aid, Panchayat raj, Family Welfare and Population Control, Prevention of AIDS, Science for the Masses, Environment Protection, Legal Literacy, National Integration, Cookery, and A Course for Integrated Family Needs.

The Department introduced a two-year MA in Continuing Education and Extension Work

The Department has also established an **e-learning Centre** that offers a Certificate Course in Functional and Communicative English; it has also designed a special course in Computer Applications with a view to encouraging students to find work dealing with development of websites and e-learning packages.

The Department has established Student Counseling/ Placement/Career Guidance Centres in various Department of the University.

The Department has been undertaking a great deal of networking activities with national and international agencies that specialize in the programme interests being evolved and pursued by it. It has established collaborative relationship with the following national agencies:

- Gorakhpur Environmental Action Group,
- Gorakhpur Environmental Protection Society,
- Yuva Chetna Samiti,
- DDRC Manav Seva Sansthan,
- Literacy Centre, Doharighat, Azamgarh,
- National Society for Equal Opportunity for the Handicapped in UP,
- Indian Adult Education Association, and
- Indian University Association for Continuing Education.

The Department received the UNESCO-NLM Award 2002 for the outstanding contribution in the field of Adult and Continuing Education. The citation for the Award noted that the Department had actively participated in the implementation of the TLC, Gorakhpur.

"—. It has established good networking with government and non-government organizations, international and domestic corporate bodies and autonomous institutions. The Department has conducted many innovative activities in areas such as Self-Help Group organization, formation of Women Cooperatives, Counseling Centre for students and adolescent groups, lecture series on development issues, communication, skill development, training in technical and vocational skills, fashion designing course, and beauty care programmes."

4.4 Summary

The Indian Universities remained an exclusive preserve of the resource-plus groups of society by narrowing their functions to teaching and research. The knowledge-generation resources available to these institutions through the research activity and the knowledge-dissemination skills through the teaching programmes were not utilized for even advocacy initiatives in support of the rights of the poor and the disadvantaged groups to access development rights and entitlements created for them.

These institutions could thus be said to have indirectly supported "Exclusion" by confining themselves to teaching and research within their campuses. Even when these institutions were located in geographic areas and socio-economic environments that were characterized by widespread poverty, illiteracy, discrimination against women, and, biases against the Scheduled Castes and the Scheduled Tribes, it was only when a fiat was issued from the top (i.e. the University Grants Commission) that they moved towards committing their resources to eradication of illiteracy, universalization of elementary education, and provision of Continuing Education programmes.

The Universities participated in the first mass programme for eradication of illiteracy in the form of the National Adult Education Programme by involving both their students and teachers. Such participation triggered concerns with various other issues including poverty and backwardness of the people, low levels of health in poverty and backward pockets, and, absence of equity and justice in access to planned development resources.

The intellectual potential available with these institutions resulted in several new educational programmes that were rooted in the development programmes and processes.

5

Linking Literacy and Adult Education with Development

5.1 Literacy as an Instrument in Development

Adult education is polyvalent by nature since the nature of an adult learner's universe of interests or concerns is limitless. **Literacy and Adult Education** is planned responses to a diverse set of needs of the adult learners. **Literacy and Adult Education** should be concerned with the whole life of the adult learners – for self, at home, at work and in the community. The content of b should thus be all-embracing and inevitably must represent a vast web of activities.

Literacy and Adult Education could thus include

- *General Education* (Literacy, Numeracy, Living Skills, Civics and Social Studies, etc.),
- *Vocational Training*,
- *Civic and Social Education* covering individual interests, the family, the community, and, socio-cultural concerns.

Coombs (1973) opined that the "purpose of basic general education for men and women is to offer them precisely essential experiences to enable them to participate in the modern world with greater confidence and improved chances of success. The ingredients are the acquisition of positive attitudes, sufficient functional literacy and numeracy to read with comprehension a national newspaper or magazine— to write a legible letter — — and to handle important common computations — a scientific outlook and an elementary understanding of the processes of nature, functional knowledge and skills for earning a living, functional knowledge and skills for civic participation."

Literacy has been viewed as a set of skills that can bring information and knowledge concerning both the development process and the opportunities made available under that process to the people of any given area. A number of studies have provided evidence to suggest the existence of "mutual analytical and empirical linkages between human resources and poverty in India." Acquisition of literacy skills and performance in education, especially in case of girls and women, appear to be closely related to their health and fertility behaviour. It has also been suggested that "female literacy and workforce participation are important determinants of variations in child mortality." It has been observed that "better educated women are more likely to marry late, exercise greater control over the choice of size of family, have fewer children and adopt family planning methods on a larger scale".

A **World Bank study (1997)** has revealed that "the offer price for labour improves with the health and educational attainments of the labour force". **Jayagopal (1985)** refers to a group of World Bank studies that assert "a high correlation between adult literacy and development"; the very process of learning has thus been considered critical for participation in the development process in any society.

Jayagopal (1985) suggests a link between "quality of life" and literacy. He states the following:

"It is estimated, for instance, that among the factors that account for economic growth, education contributed 11.1 percent in Asia and 17.2 percent in Africa. There is also a clear correlation between literacy rates and the economic performance of countries for the period 1960-77, the eight fastest growing countries had 16 percent higher literacy rates than the average for the developing countries as a whole and achieved a 5.7 percent growth rate as against 2.4 percent for all LDCs. One computation has it that an increase of 20 percentage points in the literacy rate is associated with a 0.5 percent higher growth rate. The impact of education is not limited to GNP growth but extends to all aspects of social welfare. It has been found to have positive, measurable influence on life expectancy and a one percent increase in literacy is associated with a reduction in infant mortality by 0.55 percent per 1000 of the population." (p. 2)

Dubashi (1983) undertook the task of constructing the Composite Quality of Life Index that measures the welfare aspects. It incorporated three aspects of welfare, namely (1) life expectancy, (2) infant mortality, and (3) basic literacy.

The **Education Commission (1966)** observed that the "circumstances of modern life condemn the illiterate to live an inferior existence"; he has little prospects of reasonable income.

Jalaluddin (1980) believed that in order to highlight the links between literacy and development what has often been ignored are the **social and political dimensions of literacy and adult education programmes** in countries where the illiteracy rate and the level of social and economic deprivation are still very high. He elaborates his point in the following words:

"—. Most of these countries are also faced with the threatening growth of population and its accompanying adverse effects. However, it has been the experience of several countries of the world that literacy and continuing education campaigns, when organized as a mass movement, may take the form of social reform of historic importance in the life of a nation. Such campaigns also go a long way in reducing social tensions through ensuring greater participation of the weaker sections of the society in the process of economic and social development. In fact, wherever the literacy and adult education campaigns have succeeded, they proved to be great factors facilitating political socialization and accelerated self-development and self-management of the traditionally weaker sections of the society." (p. 2-3)

Uttar Pradesh continued, for long, to be a state where "educational access has remained confined to upper caste males; the spread of education among socially disadvantaged groups and women has extremely significant implications for the economic progress of these groups.

Participation by women in Panchayat Raj Institutions has tended to be somewhat shaky on account of widespread illiteracy among them. It has been observed that the "absence of widespread literacy is a serious obstacle in empowering women and socially disadvantaged groups who have acquired the possibility of taking responsibility of formal leadership in the various rungs of self-government." Absence of literacy makes it difficult for them to undertake social audit of development programmes in their area, both at the planning and implementation stages. The officials connected with such programmes do not feel compelled to maintain transparency and people's participation both in the process of planning and implementation.

Chambers (1995) affirms this view when he states that education impacts directly on virtually on all dimensions of deprivation (physical, social, economic, political and psychological).

Olson and Torrance ((**2001**) prefer to use the term "social literacy" for the above perspectives. They articulate the following view:

"— A literate society is not just a society in which a majority of people know how to read and write; it is a society in which important aspects of social life such as economics, law, science, and government are organized around texts and document to form what we may call "textual institutions." Personal literacy allows one to participate in such institutions but personal literacy in itself does not guarantee the creation of such institutions nor their effectiveness. Literacy campaigns around the world failed, it was argued, because they focused on personal literacy but failed to come to grips with the problem of social literacy. Social literacy refocuses the problem on to the development of and participation in textual practices of an increasingly bureaucratic society. An understanding of literacy must include how individuals and groups adopt and utilize writing in the pursuit of their goals, whether organizing a cooperative, filing a land claim, or publishing a narrative. But it must include how individuals and groups come to terms with such textual practices of the dominant bureaucratic institutions of a literate society. A theory of literacy and social development must bring into relief such facts as that being able to read and write a contract is worthless unless there are institutions such as courts to enforce them. Thus issues of literacy are not independent of issues of power. Such considerations help to explain why literacy activities sometimes become self-sustaining and why, more often, literacy programs in both developed and developing countries failed.

To bridge the personal and the institutional it is necessary to think of literacy as an instrumental rather than a causal factor in social development. This perspective focuses the question on how people can use literacy as an instrument in the achievement of personal and collective goals ranging from forming a personal identity to organizing economic reforms. Literacy is thus subordinated to activities and goals without being lost as a decisive instrument in social development." (pp. xi-xi)

Sachchidananda, et al (1991) evaluated the Project on Radio Education for Adult Literacy (PREAL) in Hiropatti of Madhubani District; they found that the women learners came in increasing numbers from the backward and Scheduled Caste families. The women learners liked learning through Radio; while the average attendance on normal days was from 9 to 12, it increased during the days when Radio was utilized for the learning process. Attendance on days when the Radio was utilized shot up to 15. the women learners appeared to have become more self-confident and assertive. There appeared to be a more positive orientation towards personal hygiene and cleanliness in their households than before. However, only one-third of the participants in this learning process continued till the end; the novelty of the media use in the learning process became a source of initial attraction; however, the novelty soon wore out.

5.2 Illiteracy and the Diversity of Poverty Settings

Triebel (2001) argues that literacy is at best an instrument in enabling people to seek development resources, an instrument that might facilitate the process of change in their lives. Literacy by itself does not cause a change in their lives, leave along the larger paradigm of social change. "Literacy may play a significant instrumental role in psychological and social change in some cultural and institutional contexts." By itself, literacy helps to preserve and accumulate "development information"; societies require institutional and cultural contexts (laws and their enforcement, accountability of the governance systems, enforcement of democratic rights, etc.).

5.2.1 Literacy in Slum Settings

In slum settings, literacy would be perceived as a meaningful instrument if it plays a critical role in family practices, communication with the local self-government mechanisms, articulation of personal or group identity, building social capital in the local area, accessing employment in the unorganized/informal sector, etc. Slums continue to be, by and large, oral societies frequently mediated by intermediate functionaries helping to establish links with the functioning of complex bureaucratic structures. These could be seen in terms of scribes helping to write letters outside the post office, persons helping with the filling of applications for ration cards, complaints to the police authorities, etc.

Have literacy initiatives reached a dead end in the urban slums? The literacy planners in India are still struggling to formulate a system of literacy programme delivery in the urban slums. The **National Literacy Mission** found it administratively feasible to rely on the role that the Collector played in a district as the Chairman of the District Literacy Committee. The technical resource support providing agencies (e.g., the State Resource Centre, the District Resource Unit, and the Block Resource Unit) handled the preparation and distribution of literacy learning materials and other requirements keeping in view the predominantly rural background of the population. Agricultural and agri-industries provided the somewhat uniform thematic background for both the content and instructional strategies for the learning materials. However, the urban slums comprise of socio-culturally diverse groups characterized by some amount of external solidarity, but marked internal differentiation. Most urban slums house residents from different linguistic and ethnic groups, living with their own languages, kinship systems, dress styles and food habits. Slums are not administratively marked out in any city in India; there is no separate administrative system for slums per se, though there is a Slums Wing that plans for and responds to development constraints experienced by slums with a city as a whole. The **National Literacy Mission** has at best been exploring the multiple dimensions of an Urban Literacy Project, rather than a slum-specific literacy project.

There is need to undertake studies to assess the extent of use of reading and writing in slums both in the personal and social life of the slum dwellers. Such assessment of use of reading and writing skills in slums should be further analyzed in terms of their criticality in the growth of "literate institutions" (e.g. ration card office, births and deaths registration office, marriage registration office, complaints office for water, electricity, sanitation, drainage, fire station, floods control, shops and establishments registration office, licence for selling goods and wares on pavements in the weekly markets, etc.) leading to the emergence of "societal literacy". Politicians and other power brokers have held back a great deal of development information from the poor with the intention of selectively releasing the same at times of survival crises in the lives of the poor; an institutional framework for right to information would empower the poor to make use of such development information in accessing their legitimate development rights without the help of any intermediaries.

Literacy is embedded in a system of social functions and cultural processes; mere alphabetical competence is at best a technical skill, not necessarily requiring frequent use. It has often been pointed out that a literate society is not made of "training everyone into readers and writers; it requires the invention or development of literate institutions".

Some NGOs have openly voiced the view that the strategy for working towards universal literacy in urban slums ought to be through "technicracy", i.e. provision of technical skills linked to the process of enhancing employability of workers in the unorganized sector on the one hand, and, accessing development entitlements and disaster relief on the other. Others believe that literacy in urban slums could evoke an enthusiastic ownership provided it is soaked in "social negotiation skills" aimed at enabling slum dwellers to seek solutions to their survival problems or gaps in their life through an organized access to their development rights.

Verma (2002) points out that the Indian Railways owns some 4.2 lakh hectares of land, mostly in narrow strips along tracks; such land is home to "a sizable section of the slum population". She traces the emergence of slums to the phenomenon of "inequitable land distribution; its root cause seems to lie "not in urban poverty, but in urban wealth". The slum people are often denied their fundamental rights (the right to shelter, right to resettlement, and the right to minimum services) largely on account of a surreptitious emergence of a "shadow charter of rights" in urban development practices to ensure inequity.

Adult literacy campaigns have drawn poor response largely on account of their predominant focus on personal literacy or on mere promises of social and economic gains; these have to find content and learning methodologies from the processes that help slum groups develop into communities (sharing internal and external solidarity goals), expansion of local markets and increased social integration at the inter-slum level and at levels across the slums in the larger democratic polity. Literacy in slum settings needs to be embedded in the vast network of denials that socio-economic structures have created against the slum dwellers.

5.2.2 Literacy in Rural Settings

The rural poor continue to live in conditions of abject poverty; the Constitutional Right to Life with Dignity is still a pipe dream. The rural poor invariably tend to be landless, illiterate, and lack purchasing power to be able to buy food even from the Targeted Public Distribution System (TPDS). Other factors like caste, gender and geographic location worsen their poverty condition. While in most places they suffer from landlessness, there are places where they do not have access to water either for irrigation or for domestic consumption. In places where they have land and water, the productivity of land is quite low on account of lack of credit to acquire the agricultural inputs or on account of lack of awareness concerning and access to new technologies or improved farming practices on the one hand and employment generation possibilities from diversified agriculture on the other. The agricultural extension processes are at their poorest level in pockets having concentration of the rural poor. Such services are grossly inadequate at the level of the small and marginal farmers, landless labourers (who undertake sharecropping operations), and women. In some pockets of Uttar Pradesh, farmers are able to produce only 25 quintal of wheat per ha. as against 38 in Haryana and 40 in Punjab. Similarly, the average cropping intensity in Uttar Pradesh is 124 percent as against 300 percent in the other areas.

Numerous accounts of rural poverty have thus been documented from villages in eastern parts of Uttar Pradesh, Bundelkhand, and, Uttrakhand. The political elites tend to overstress the relevance of political solution to such conditions of rural poverty and extreme backwardness; they believe that creation of small states could enable people to determine their own development processes. However, such solutions are perceived to be a problem since these cause an excessive strain on the scarce public resources. The political and bureaucratic elites often become the sole beneficiaries of such political situations.

Efforts should be made to explore the possibility of sound economic solutions by which the poor can access their development rights at the lowest possible intermediation costs. What can be planned and implemented at the local level need not invite intervention even from the next higher level, leave alone the state or the national levels. The political and bureaucratic elites must learn to minimize their anxieties and fears emanating from the emergence of strong village level democratic institutions capable of planning and implementing development. The size of government appears, unfortunately, to be in inverse relation to the possibility of development of and by the poor.

There appears, however, to be considerable hope for the rural poor in areas where the agricultural extension services have developed strong outreach capabilities in the often remote pockets of rural and tribal areas. It has led to small attempts at diversification of agriculture resulting in remarkable progress in livestock development (the milk plus movement), horticulture, sericulture, etc. This movement has been further supported by land planning and watershed development helping reclamation of even wasteland. In some areas the practice of Joint Forest Management has placed some segments of the rural poor in control of planning and use of the forest produce; however, it is often confined to the planning and use of degraded land areas. The Village Forest and Development Committees in Himachal Pradesh, for example, have yet to address the village development function.

The rural poor have invariably been either denied or deprived of the minimum basic needs including shelter, sanitation, clean drinking water, health care services, and, literacy and education. The comparatively higher infant mortality rates in conditions of extreme poverty have often spurred high fertility rates resulting in high birth rates. There is practically no provision for pre-school education in poverty pockets in the rural areas. It has not been possible to provide for Universal Primary Education for all children in the age group 6 - 11 years, leave alone Universal Elementary Education for all the children in the age group 6 - 14 years. In fact, the State appears to be altogether abandoning the use of the phrase "Universal Elementary Education" by replacing it with "Universal Primary Education" to lower the commitment which it made in the **Constitution of India**. The Government of India now believes that it requires Rs. 1,37,00 crores to be able to fulfill the commitment of even Universal Primary Education.

The rural poor, particularly the rural poor women, are forced to value the health of their animals (in many cases, probably their only assets) more than the health of their family members. Faced with the dilemma of a sick animal and a sick adult or child member in their families, the invariable first choice for health care attention goes in favour of the animal, rather than the family member. Women's and girls' health, in particular, often suffered the worst forms of neglect. Women's and girls' education also encounters similar neglect.

Wherever the poor have been enabled to find sustainable livelihoods, they have taken positive decisions in support of literacy and adult education for themselves, education for their children, including the girl children. Health care and education have become priorities for them in such contexts. However, child labour practices often form part of the quest for sustainable livelihoods by the rural poor. The phenomenon of seasonal employment opportunities forces them to look for alternate employment opportunities during the somewhat prolonged lean periods of economic activity. While the Government of India estimates such lean periods to be of the duration of approximately 100 days, the period is much longer in case of many rural and tribal areas.

The worst and the most critical area of social development is the very low extent of organized behaviour among communities of the rural poor. The diverse initiatives aimed at formation of Self-Help Groups (SHGs) and other organizations of the poor appear to have created some hope for a Rights Perspective to access development by and among the poor. The movement towards organized behaviour could pick up considerable speed if the Civil Society groups strive for more cultural and political space for Self-Help action.

The rural poor often lack access to or use of existing marketing infrastructure; the middlemen often manage to block their effective functioning in the market. Even where government-directed support price mechanisms have been brought into operation, delays in payment for procured crops have often forced the rural poor to undersell their crops and other produce to the middlemen. The extensive marketing infrastructural mechanisms and other forms of support to Horticultural activity in Himachal Pradesh is an example to be appropriately considered by Uttar Pradesh, particularly for its hill and mountain areas.

The access to credit is another significant movement which has grown from the level of the villages. The rural poor in diverse parts of the country have come together to form more than a lakh of thrift and credit groups pooling their own small savings and providing credit, often for economically productive purposes, to their members without recourse to the lengthy and cumbersome procedures insisted upon by the formal banking sector. The formal banking sector appears to have responded to this large market for retail credit by creating mechanisms through such institutions as NABARD and SIDBI. Such institutions are attempting to convert such village-based Credit and Thrift Groups into Self-Help Groups and have them linked to the banks for access to credit.

Attempts by The NABARD, SIDBI, and even other Banks to enter the emerging retail markets have, in fact, their new strategy to maintain their profitability in view of the falling interest rates globally. They are equally anxious to widen the client base of the existing 153000 retail credit outlets (in the form of Primary Agricultural Credit Societies, Regional Rural Banks, and, the Commercial Banks). However, such institutions have not yet recognized the need to facilitate low-cost access to credit by the rural poor. Their management orientations are still corporate and high-cost in nature, and, consequently unsuited to the present economic conditions of the poor.

The situation implies that the cost of managing an NGO is three times less than that of managing a Commercial Bank for providing services to the rural poor. It further reveals that the intermediation costs of reaching credit to the rural poor are three to four times higher than the original amount provided by these institutions. The situation is far from being a low-cost delivery of resources and services to the poor. Where NGOs strive to have direct access to credit resources from NABARD with a view to reducing intermediation costs, the provision of a sound corporate or institutional guarantee is invoked. The provisions of the Stamp Duty Act also run counter to the effective group functioning of the NGOs in the micro-credit movement.

Such criticism not withstanding, both NABARD and SIDBI can further fine-tune their pro-poor role in facilitating access to credit and other business development services. Both these institutions need to evolve a "credit plus" framework by evolving mechanisms for services to support backward and forward linkages in both production and marketing for the micro-enterprises initiated by the rural poor through access to credit.

The rural poor have not been provided the opportunity for sustained participation at any of the levels of governance -

village, block, district, state or national - in the country. The electoral process creates an occasional threat for the governing elites (both political and bureaucratic) to recognize and respond to the needs of the rural poor, however, even such threats are rarely allowed to be converted into opportunities for the poor to participate in and influence the governance processes in terms of planning for and implementation of the village development priorities and processes.

The governance processes dare to be almost indifferent to the problems of the poor since elements of transparency in and accountability of utilization of public resources are frequently ignored. The Right to Information, or the Right to Monitoring of Development Programmes by the Poor, or the Right to Povertywatch or Social Audit are issues which evoke, at best, occasional public rhetoric with no substantive action. In fact, the governance processes attempt to resort to counter allegations against the Civil Society groups in the wake of demands for transparency in and accountability.

The middle classes are increasingly staying away from both the democratic and governance processes; they seem to recognize that reliance on such institutions is often misplaced. However, the poor in tribal, rural and urban areas still seem to have a great deal of faith in and hope from both the democratic and governance processes. Both these processes and the mechanisms need to respond to the rights of the poor.

The above stated profiling of the poor in rural areas clearly indicates that the poor

- have some assets and resources which need to be revitalized for enhanced productivity,
- need some missing resources (land, water, credit, production and marketing skills, temporary safety nets to find a place in the market),

- appear to have a better chance to assert their place in the community and the market through organized beahiour manifest in formation and management of their own organizations,
- with access to new or upgraded work skills, are able to find enhanced income levels and take decisions supportive of community goals,
- need access to technologies and improved work practices,
- must be encouraged to participate in democratic fora for governance to facilitate the articulation and audibility of the voices of the poor, and
- can achieve social development goals when efforts are initiated in conjunction with economic development processes.

The profiling of the poor also suggests that indicators for Povertywatch need to be developed in the context of diversity of poverty conditions in India and be incorporated as content in literacy and adult education programmes. The povertywatch indicators could include the following:

- sense of solidarity and organization among the rural poor as manifest in the frequency of their meetings, extent of participation, issues deliberated upon, etc.,
- accountability of community leadership,
- right to own/manage local resources,
- recognition and practice of gender equity as manifest in number of women in paid employment and number of women as community leaders,
- extent of negotiation initiated by the community through its leadership with the local self-government,

- growth in the extent of absorption or utilization of development resources earmarked for the areas,
- changes in skills (upgradation as relevant to local market needs), technology practices, and, implements/tools upgradation,
- extent to which informal or unorganized sector participants have been integrated with formal sector mechanisms (Banks, Women's Development Corporations, SC/ST Development Corporations, District Industries Centres, Rural Development Programmes, etc.), and
- extent of increase in the community share of trade at the local and regional market levels as part of the community's progress towards integrating the micro with the macro-economy.

Both the Universities and NGOs should work together to develop the following training programmes in the form of short-term courses for the grassroots workers:

- Formation and Management of Self-Help Groups at the village level,
- Formation and Management of Federations of village-based Self-Help Groups,
- Participatory and People-led Formulation of Village Development Plan,
- Participation in Local Self-Government (PRIs) for local Socio-economic Development,
- Planning and Managing a Rural Micro-enterprise,
- Joint Forest Management,

- Formulating a Human Development Report at the Village Level,
- Networking with Local Government and Other Development Institutions,
- Advocacy Local Government, Business Groups, and Media for Pro-Poor Processes,
- Advocacy for Voluntary Efforts in Development Planning and Implementation,
- Social Audit of Poverty Alleviation Programmes at Village, Block and District Levels,
- University-NGO Interaction with the State Governments: Annual Plans and Annual Budget, and
- Rural Poverty: Perspectives of the Rural Poor.

Universities and NGOs could also generate and disseminate local language-based documentation on the following subjects:

- Pro-Poor Development Programmes at the District Level,
- Formation and Management of Self-Help Groups,
- Formation and Management of Federation of Self-Help Groups,
- A Charter of Rights for Small and Marginal Farmers, Landless Labourers and Artisans,
- Planning and Managing a Micro-enterprise,
- Planning and Managing a Watershed Programme in the Village,

- Planning and Managing a Local Seed Bank,
- Participation by the Rural Poor in the Marketing Processes,
- Mobilizing Resources for a Local Area Economic Infrastructure,
- Formulating a Village Development Plan by the Rural Poor,
- Social Audit of Rural Development at Gram Sabha, Panchayat Samiti and Zila Parishad,
- Enhancing Gender Equity in the Rural Economy,
- Integration of and Convergence Among Pro-Poor Development Efforts in a Village,
- Forming Pro-poor Partnership with the Local Bank,
- Subsidies and the Rural Poor,
- Pro-poor Advocacy for the State Annual Plan,
- Pro-poor Advocacy for the State Annual Budget,
- Human Development Report of a Village, and
- Regional Experiences in Micro-credit in India.

Universities could also undertake the following activities:

- Initiate area-specific planning and implementation for universal literacy and universal primary education in pockets of low enrollment and retention,
- Initiate awareness activities aimed at propagating acceptance of the small family norm and facilitating access to quality health services,

- Initiate area-specific activities aimed at facilitating diversification of agriculture,

- Initiate the process of large scale formation of Self-Help Groups to mobilize local savings, access institutional credit, and support micro-enterprise planning and development with profit,

- initiate assessment of initiatives in people's participation in planned development (Village Forest and Development Committees, Village Education Committees, etc.) in terms of the extent of democratic participation, functions-resources linkage, and transparent behavioural practices, and

- plan advocacy sessions on pro-poor issues and concerns involving universities, NGO, media, other professions for the people, and the government.

5.3 Economic Development and Literacy

Advocacy for pro-poor rights essentially involves

- articulating people's demand for, access to and utilization of services (e.g., health, education) and their access to the means of production.

- securing commitment of the state, the local authority, and the community for the eradication of poverty, and

- lobbying for mechanisms which facilitate increase in household disposable income including actions that create new employment opportunities, democratize access to credit and set up income generation activities for women.

- The conditions of the poor could be seen in three specific stages:

- **survival needs** of the poor which are common to all poor irrespective of their geographic location - food, clean drinking water, shelter, health, and, environmental sanitation,

- **well-being and development needs** which facilitate their sustained survival through Self-Help development initiatives - literacy and education, ownership of minimum assets in terms of land, livestock, access to work with a wage ensuring dignified survival, and

- **empowerment needs** whereby the poor form organizations to take participatory and consensus-based decisions concerning Self-Help development initiatives, sustenance of such organizations of the poor, accessing rights to participate in the planning and implementation of their own development, accessing rights to povertywatch the development processes, and informed participation in the governance processes.

The **first priority in pro-poor advocacy ought to be accorded to the survival needs of the poor** to ensure that no citizen is rendered vulnerable to the indignities of hunger and starvation, disease on account of lack of access to clean drinking water, harmful exposure to the elements of Nature or man-made vagaries on account of lack of minimum shelter needs, or in conditions of filth and squalor which threaten human health. Such situations must call for a priority allocation of development resources, participatory and people-led formulation of plans and implementation of programmes.

The second and third levels of poverty - **well-being** and **development needs**, and, **empowerment needs** - appear to vary with the geographic contexts in which the poor are currently placed - hill and mountain areas, desert areas, coastal areas, and, plains areas. The **well-being and development needs** of the poor are sought to be responded through the various poverty alleviation programmes. The advocacy framework for this category of needs must be thus seen in the relevance of the policy framework to the diverse groups of the poor and the degree to which participation of the poor is encouraged in the implementation processes. A critical and informed review of the policy and programmes duly supplemented with case studies drawn from the diverse geographic situations must become the content of such advocacy. It should give rise to enhanced legislative time and qualitative discussion on the pro-poor issues in the appropriate bodies and their sub-structures.

The **empowerment needs perspective** on the lives of the poor has given rise to inculcation of organized behaviour among the poor leading to formation of first level organizations of the poor in tribal settlements, villages and in urban slums. Many of these organizations continue to be informal in nature; a second level growth in such organized behaviour needs to be facilitated through access to legal status for such organizations, formation of federations of such organizations, and their linkage with district, state and national level mechanisms which facilitate access to missing resources (appropriate technologies, credit, business development services, etc.).

The support to the legislative process could take the form of the much-needed technical inputs to facilitate informed and ground-level realities in the deliberative processes. The information resources (in the form of reports, case studies, and evaluation reports) generated from the grassroots level ought to be converted in the form of **Questions, Calling Attention Motions**, even **Committee presentations**.

Advocacy must initiate expansion of political space within which Assessment-Analysis-Action processes could be initiated and sustained at diverse levels. It must, in its ultimate analysis, provide people with choices and the ability to choose, as well as to gain more control over resources they need to improve their condition. It must influence service delivery processes, social mobilization processes, and help to achieve time-bound goals.

Decentralization has increased poor people's participation primarily in cases where service delivery has either been turned over to the local bodies or where the Civil Society groups including the NGOs have initiated innovative service delivery mechanisms. Some of the evidence presented suggests that the Poor's participation is most effective when two additional conditions are met:

(a) the poor are free to associate and organize at the local level; and

(b) the local body responsible for managing service delivery is elected by the community.

Eliminating corruption requires bureaucratic reforms that guarantee transparency and accountability in the management of public resources and information and accountability of public officials. To achieve this, some efforts are being made to articulate demand for right to information; at other places **Jan Sunwais** are being held to let the local people speak up on development projects initiated in their local areas. Others suggest involving the media in making public officials account for decisions and establishing public fora for addressing citizens' grievances.

The size and scale of governments continues to be inimical to the expanded role of the poor and their social institutions. The space for community-based and effective governance appears to be characterized by an inverse relationship with the size and scale of the governmental structures. The answer perhaps seems to lie in still greater pressure from the community-based institutions, still greater participation by the poor in the political process, and, global support to pro-poor policies and programmes.

The critical question in our understanding of the poor lies in the choice we make of the **development milieu**: should it be the **urban-preferred aggressive and highly individualized instinct for progress**, or, should it be **community-conscious, compassion-led, and limits-to-human-needs perspectives of the poor**? We ought to devote research attention to the vision of human development as imbibed and cherished by the poor, to the loss of human energy in the pursuit of urban-cherished individualism (since the poor still remain at the scantiest fringe of urban society even after migration from the rural areas), and, the reasons for the impoverishment of the rural resources entailed by the urban prescriptions for development.

The critical need for the raising or growth of social capital in India is preferentially seen in the agricultural sector, particularly among the landless labourers, women in agriculture, small and marginal farmers, etc. India has 77 percent of her population living in rural areas; agriculture accounts for more than 27 percent of the Gross Domestic Product. The rural sector provides employment to nearly 243 million people constituting nearly 70 percent of the labour force. The lot of the poor is closely tied to the fate of the rural sector and its employment opportunities; it determines to a large extent the country's quest for sustained poverty reduction, food security, and even the size of the market for industry and services.

Social capital formation processes could support the growth of the **rural non-farm sector** as the additional area for augmenting employment opportunities - particularly in livestock development, forestry and fisheries, and, in services (construction, trade, finance, transport, repairs and maintenance, education, health, self-governance, etc.). A great deal of pressure is being exerted by the international institutions to reduce governmental role in providing access to such services; private sector participation is being advocated both for input distribution and service provision. It is an issue of research to assess if the private sector participation would substantially be driven by market demand or if it would have empathy with the social goal of reaching such inputs and services to the poor. The international agencies are probably rushing us into such situations without waiting to assess the impact of such market-led changes on the poor.

The pro-poor research concerns warrant that university segments which have substantive interest in the communities of the poor or in areas with concentration of the poor devote attention to some of the following issues:

- **leakages in the implementation of the poverty alleviation programmes,**

- **extent of mobilization among the poor (both in terms of organized behaviour and in terms of savings) through the Self-Help groups** and the use of such savings for both individual and group micro-enterprise development,

- **area-specific social audit of wage income** distributed under the Jawahar Rozgar Yojana with a view to enhancing the percentage of resource transfer to the poor,

- **appropriateness of assets created and their sustained** to the economic and social infrastructural needs of the area,

- **role of the Gram Panchayats in planning and implementation of rural employment programmes,**

- **role of the NGOs as implementing and monitoring agencies in the poverty alleviation programmes,** and

- **extent of administrative efficiency of the District Rural Development Agency** in the planning and implementation of the poverty alleviation programmes.

5.4 Youth as Pro-Development Change Agents

The Universities and Colleges could gainfully work towards strengthening the role of literacy as an instrument for development by first planning some initiatives that enable them to control their own lives with confidence. Young people facing crises themselves cannot facilitate responses to change in the lives of others.

The young people today, particularly those on the threshold of leaving senior secondary schools and stepping into the larger society and the market as active participants and without the shelter of their parents and teachers, face a world that assures them of tremendous resources and power – through access to parental wealth sans time, to technology, an environment that emboldens their capacity to dream and aspire for themselves and for those around them, and an exuberant psychological state of mind that eggs them on to challenge, if not altogether throw aside, the range of "do's and don'ts" formally or informally enforced by their parents, teachers and the immediate society around them. Such resources and power with the youth vary based on their geographic location – urban, rural, and tribal in that order. Within urban areas, the access to resources and power varies based on the location of their residential and work environments – organized sector offices and well-developed colonies, the lower middle class colonies and lower income group housing colonies, and, the slums and kutcha hutments. Despite such resources and power available to them in varying measures, most young people experience hesitations in such matters as **handling personal lives in the domain of interpersonal relationships, finding space for themselves in the modern society, coping with pressures created by globalization of the market and**

the media, and **accessing the new and emerging markets for utilization of their knowledge and skills**.

It is doubtful if the schools and any other informal or non-formal education programmes supported by the family and the community raise such issues in their curricular or co-curricular initiatives. Most of them wake up to the situation when aberrations suddenly burst upon the social scene – e.g., young people found drinking in school premises, floating/ hacking a website with pornographic intents targeting their peer group, wittingly or unwittingly circulating video clips of sexual postures within their peer group, committing rape on a female person passing through a lonely area, committing suicide on account of failure to cope with academic achievement pressures created by parents and others in the peer group, stretching anxiety and depression on account of failure in the market to ending their lives, etc.

It is in this context that a felt need exists for articulating the need for planning and undertaking **Readiness for Life Education Programme** as part of the co-curricular activity stream, or of the informal education initiatives within the community, or of the distance education initiatives. The Departments of Adult, Continuing Education & Extension in the Universities need to adopt a pro-institutional youth programming policy as a first step to seeking a commitment from the youth for support to Universal Literacy initiatives linked with development.

- **Handling personal lives in the domain of interpersonal relationships,**
- **Finding space for themselves in the modern society,**
- **Coping with the vision of being a global citizen,** and
- **Accessing the new and emerging markets for utilization of their knowledge and skills.**

The education sector is expected to facilitate development and recognition of "competencies" that comprise a wide range of behavioural skills, work-related knowledge and technical including the need to expand skill development activities that prepare workers for self-employment. The process of formal education and training is becoming less one of passing on information and more one of individuals "learning to learn" so that they can find out for themselves. It is not just the "knowledge about facts", but the need "to learn how to access, analyze and exploit information and transform it into new knowledge".

Such an educational programme could comprise of the following:

- **Basic (foundation) education for all**: this should include such areas as (i) need for literacy, numeracy, and techniracy; (ii) citizenship, (iii) social skills, (iv) learning-to-learn skills, (v) the ability to solve personal and group/community problems together, etc.

- **Core work skills for all**: this should include (i) creativity, (ii) personal effectiveness (self-esteem, goal-setting, and motivation, skills for personal and career development), (iii) group effectiveness (interpersonal, teamwork, and negotiation skills), (iii) organizational effectiveness and leadership skills, (iv) labour market navigation skills (job search skills, presenting oneself to prospective employers, identifying career options and opportunities, and, identifying and evaluating jobs and education and training programme opportunities), and (v) familiarity with the Internet.

- **Lifelong learning for all**: this should call for (i) recognition of the centrality of the learner, catering to a diversity of learner needs, emphasis on the motivation to learn (through self-paced, and self-directed and increasingly ICT-assisted learning), (ii) continuing improvement in skills and competencies as work, technology and skill requirements change, etc.

It would require elaboration of the content areas, getting together a panel of experts to support presentation of the content and promote interaction thereon, and conversion of the content in the identified medium for its presentation and transmission.

Appendix - I

Tenth Five Year Plan UGC Guidelines on Adult, Continuing Education, Extension and Field Outreach

1. Introduction

1.1 As one traces the recommendations of the various Commissions and the UGC guidelines issued from time to time for Adult, Continuing Education and Extension, it is evident that one of the goals of the UGC is to transform the university system into an active instrument for social change through the institutionalization of Extension as the Third Dimension and by ensuring that the university system is adult learner friendly and pro-life long learning.

1.2 It is commonly known that through the dimension of teaching, there is dissemination of knowledge, through research new knowledge is generated and through the dimension of extension there is application of knowledge in real life situations, which leads to the further generation of new knowledge.

1.3 It was way back in 1960 that the Kothari Commission first articulated the concept of Extension and the TRINITY of Teaching, Research and Extension. The Commission stated that Extension was essential for:

- making education relevant to real life situations

- for preventing the alienation of the educand from society
- for developing in the educand a sense of responsibility towards society
- for deepening the teacher's knowledge through a wider exposure to real life situations

1.4 In 1977 the University Grants Commission first incorporated Extension into its Policy Statement for Higher Education when it stated that if the University system has to discharge adequately its responsibilities to the entire education system and to the society as a whole it must assume extension as the third important responsibility and give it the same status as teaching and research. This is a new and extremely significant area which should be developed on the basis of high priority.

1.5 The acceptance of Extension as the Third Dimension equal in importance to teaching and research was in the context of a growing realization that the universities and colleges having institutional resources-knowledge, manpower and physical-have an obligation to develop sensitivities to involve the development of the community with particular reference to the overall and diverse learning needs of all the segments of the people of the community.

2. Aim/Objectives

Aim

The Third Dimension was to aim at promoting a meaningful and sustained rapport between the Universities and the community.

Objectives

Firstly its objective was to extend knowledge and other institutional resources to the community and vice-versa and secondly its objective was to gain insights from a contact between knowledge resources and socio-cultural realities with a view to reflecting these in the entire curricular system of higher education including teaching and research. It was to be a two-way process between the experts and the people, an intellectual intervention in the community's living problems which need to be overcome through an educational process. It was to be that education which helped students to face life and its challenges and which created an ambience for a learning society.

3. Efforts by UGC

3.1 The opportunity to introduce the Extension Dimension in Universities was taken when the National Adult Education Programme (NAEP) was announced by the Government of India in 1978. Then Centres/ \Departments. for Adult and Continuing Education were set up in Universities. Thereafter, the Adult Education Programme as Point 16 of the 20-Point Programme of the Government of India was introduced (1983-1989) followed by the Area Based Approach Programme (1989-1992) and the Total Literacy Campaign (1992-1997) of the National Literacy Mission. In the Ninth Plan the UGC continued the Adult and Continuing Education Programme in a manner that facilitated the Centres \ Departments of Adult and Continuing Education and Extension to cast their own Plan of Action for the Extension Dimension specific to their own University.

3.2 In all, the programmes introduced by the UGC from time to time, the main focus has been on Adult Literacy, Post-literacy and field outreach programmes. Attention was given in the Ninth Plan to Adult and Continuing Education for university groups, groups that had passed the university system but had a need to return and to groups which did not have access to the university system.

3.3 In the Ninth Plan, the UGC has implemented the schemes under its Non-formal Education Bureau. As evidenced from the Gus's vision and strategy for the X Plan, the scheme will continue to be operationalised by UGC under the Non-formal Education Bureau. In order to ensure continuity, the UGC has already released grants to Departments for the years 2002?2003 and 2003-04.

4. Current Scenario

4.1 Now as the guidelines for the Tenth Plan period are being cast it is essential that the current situation, internationally and nationally, be considered. It is well known that the impact of globalization has placed new demands on the education system. Transformation with rapid change is taking place everywhere. The student and youth have to be prepared by the university to adopt change and learn new skills in accordance with the new demands of the world of work. In other words, the university system has to prepare the student to be a life long learner. Then only will the student be able to sustain his knowledge and skills at an international bench mark level.

4.2 Further private universities are being setup and international universities will soon be entering the country. Also, Information and Communication Technology (ICT) is being more frequently used in the field of learning. On-line learning and e-learning will soon become a regular feature of university courses. It is, therefore, essential that the university system and specially the Departments of Adult and Continuing Education and Extension begin to interact and collaborate with the private sector. Secondly, e-learning and the on-line mode for the conduct of courses are utilized for continuing education to cater to the needs of various sections of society including professionals.

4.3 While universities have to enhance student employability skills through a formal system, on the other hand, the non-formal stream of education is being developed by the

Ministry of Human Resource Development for reaching education to the unreached. There is a rapid growth of the National Institute of Open Schooling and State Open Schools and improvisation of quality teaching through the development of a momentum in Sarva Shiksha Abhiyan (SSA) under the Education for All programme. Universities also have to integrate formal and non-formal education by opening their doors to adult learners for life long learning programmes and by making the University an adult learner friendly institution. (Refer ? Cape Town Statement on Characteristic Elements of a Life long Learning Higher Education Institution, January 2001).

4.4 The Departments, will, therefore, have to play a more dynamic role and move from the periphery to the centre stage of the university system and to ensure this the Advisory Committees overseeing the work of the Department need to play a more pro-active role. The Departments also have to play a major role in the development of the human resource expertise in the subject of Adult, Continuing Education, Extension and Field Outreach.

4.5 At present, there are 73 Departments/Centres working in the country. As visualized earlier in the Ninth Plan, all Universities are to establish a Department for institutionalizing extension and for meeting the current demands of adult and continuing education in their respective areas of operation.

5. Thrusts

The thrusts for the Tenth Plan Period are therefore projected taking the current scenario into account. These thrusts are:-

(i) the acceptance of the philosophy of continuing education as a part of total education programme of the institution;

(ii) integration between formal and non-formal education and out of school learning processes;

(iii) reaching out to the larger sections of adults through the university system and specially deprived groups for the purpose of equalization of educational opportunities;

(iv) enrichment of the learning process of faculty and students through exposure to community needs, problems, issues and reaching out to socio-economic and cultural groups;

(v) attending to major issues relating to the National Literacy Mission, bonded labour, child-labour, street children, health conditions and issues on drugs and AIDS / HIV, nutrition, sanitation, environmental issues, gender issues with stress on gender equity, human rights education, consumer rights issues, communal harmony and cultural integration, self-employment generation and use of technology appropriate to the society;

(vi) development of the discipline of Andragogy / Adult and Continuing Education & Extension;

(vii) research for the development of theory and conduct of action research/operational research;

(viii) introduction of courses offered on campus, off campus, on-line and through e-learning;

(ix) development of courses linked specifically to business and industry which would include work ethics, work culture and preparation for the changing world of work;

(x) development of a range of credit courses at the undergraduate and postgraduate levels leading to an Associate degree in Continuing Education and;

(xi) Extension and Field Outreach to focus on

- continuing education programmes at the grassroot level through the CECs of the National Literacy Mission and through the National Institute of Open Schooling and State Open Schools;
- communal harmony and peace education;
- human rights and rights of vulnerable groups;
- environmental issues;
- panchayats and development issues;
- health education for the community and through the Health Care Centre of the university;
- women's empowerment and
- social issues and gender issues

(xii) initiating change in the policies and procedures of the university so as to make the university courses more accessible to the adult learner and

(xiii) establishing a new relationship with government organizations NGOs, Civil Societies, NGO networks and other professional bodies to address social issues.

6. Target Groups

The major target groups for the Tenth Plan period shall be:-

(i) Groups / students in the colleges and university system;

(ii) Groups who have passed out of the university system and need to return for upgradation or for the acquisition of new skills. These could include groups from industry and services;

(iii) Groups who are already in service or the underemployed or the unemployed who need to enhance their employability;

(iv) Groups which would normally not be entrants into the university system;

(v) Women, SC/ST, disadvantaged groups, street children, bonded labour, child workers, etc;

(vi) Neo-literates, CE learners, Out of school youth and

(vii) Senior citizens;

7. Programs and Activities

It is suggested that the following programs be conducted in order to cater to the needs of the different target groups. Departments can formulate the proposals by keeping the following programs in mind.

7.1 Developing the discipline of Andragogy / Adult Education and Continuing Education through academic programs and courses such as:

- Foundation Courses;
- Certificate and Diploma Courses;
- Undergraduate, postgraduate, M.Phil, Ph.D., optional/ regular courses;
- Courses integrated with different degrees such as B.Ed., M.Ed. and professional degrees;
- Projects related to continuing education and extension and field outreach in-built into a discipline of studies and
- Conduct of inter-disciplinary research in Adult, Continuing Education and Extension.

7.2 Vocational Career Oriented Courses / Programs

- Courses and programs for people at different socio-economic and educational levels for the acquisition of marketable vocational skills according to the needs and demands of urban and rural, local, national and international markets;
- Continuing education courses for the students and out of school youth;
- Courses related to the electronic media, multi media, computer applications, etc. to receive special focus;
- Apprenticeship, internship, training programs with industry and business;
- Courses specially focusing on the demands of the changing world of work;
- Para- professional courses for knowledge and skill updates and
- Career guidance for the university and college students

7.3 *Associate Degree / Diploma in Continuing Education*

Development of a credit system for courses in adult and continuing education leading to an Associate Degree / Diploma in adult and continuing education for the benefit of students who are pursuing courses on the campus.

7.4 Leadership and Human Resource Development

· Programmes for developing the potentialities of students and out of school youth, particularly of the girl students and women and

· Training of elected representatives of local, self-government, self-help groups and persons from community based organizations, NGOs, under - privileged and resource - deprived communities.

7.5 *Quality of Life Improvement Programs*

Conduct of courses and awareness programs for facilitating improvement in the quality of life of the people.

7.6 *Individual Interest Promotion Programs*

Courses and programs catering to individual interests of adults for promoting personal development.

7.7 *Social and Citizenship Role Awareness Programs*

For increasing knowledge, awareness and functional skills of the student youth and out of school youth in areas such as environment food, shelter, health, family welfare, etc. which affect them

7.8 Resource Support Programs

(i) Programs to support and evaluate TLC, PLP, CE, Sarva Shiksha Abhiyan, women's empowerment, etc. in collaboration with or for the NLM, State Literacy Mission (SLM) Zilla Sakisharta Samiti (ZSS), Centers for Women's Studies, Population Education Centres, Open Universities, People's Organizations, Community Based Organizations, Civil Societies and others.

(ii) Special programs for indigenous populations, aboriginals, slum dwellers, tribals and other vulnerable sections of society.

7.9 *Equivalency Programs*

Parallel programs offered by the Non-Formal Education Sector of the Ministry of Human Resource Development of the State and Centre, Open Schools, Institutes, etc. may be facilitated, developed and expanded.

7.10 *Academic Credit*

The work of the students involved in adult education, continuing education, extension and field outreach work should be considered for academic credit in addition to or as a part of their regular course of studies. For determining academic credits, standards may be evolved and adopted.

To illustrate:

- Projects related to extension/field outreach within a discipline at the undergraduate or postgraduate level;

- Field work in respect of a subject of study;

- Participation in literacy, post-literacy, continuing education, population education and non-formal education programs;

- Participation in programs for enhancing employability and technology skills;

- Any other activity approved for the purpose by the University Authority with the approval of the Commission.

Each University will have to determine the measures of weightage and the evaluation process for the award of an academic credit.

8. Role and Functions of the Department

8.1 *Teaching, Training and Research*

- Teaching courses in Adult and Continuing Education and Extension and Field Outreach

- Conducting need-based continuing education courses, including online courses on credit or non-credit basis;

- Conducting Orientation and Refresher courses for university and college teachers with the Academic Staff College;

- Undertaking research in the subject;
- To assist in the development of a curriculum for multi-disciplinary programs;
- To assist in the development of a library in the subject and
- Training for human resource or skill development for the different target groups

8.2 *Catalyst Role*

- Acting as a focal agency in the university system for all Extension and Field Outreach Programs with the involvement of university departments and colleges;
- Serving as a Technical Resource Centre for university's community-based activities and
- Assessing the needs of the university students and out of university learner for continuing education programs and career guidance

8.3 *Collaborative and Networking Role*

The department shall undertake collaborative programs and network with :

- business and industry;
- university departments;
- N.L.M.A;
- NGOs, Civil Society, development and government agencies and others and
- International organizations / universities and agencies, such as, UNESCO, UNICEF, UNDPA, International

Council for Adult Education, Asia South Pacific Bureau for Adult Education and similar organizations

8.4 *Documentation and Dissemination*

Publication of News Letters, journal, magazine, e-journal, creation of an interactive website, preparation of materials, dissemination of materials and information, etc.

8.5 *Monitoring and Evaluation*

Of activities and field programs of the department and of the colleges

8.6 *Facilitating Academic Departments*

to provide for Extension work through Offerings, Projects, Research, Field Activities etc.

9. Organizational Aspects

(A) Status of Departments of Adult and Continuing Education, Extension work and Field Outreach

9.1 The IX Plan guidelines have clearly stated the need for the Universities to accord a statutory status to the Departments of Adult, Continuing Education and Extension with amendments, if necessary, in the University Act and Statutes. It was also stated that the Department will have the same status as that of any other teaching department of the university with the core faculty eligible for representation on all the University bodies, like Syndicate / Executive / Management Council, Senate, Academic Council, Standing Committee on Academic Affairs, Board of Studies etc. corresponding to other University teachers. During the X Plan period, the Universities must take suitable action in this regard if such action has not been taken so far. The release of grants for the X Plan will be based on the fulfillment of this condition. In the absence of assurance from the State Govt., no vacant sanctioned post was filled.

9.2 The Department of Adult, Continuing Education and Extension and Field Outreach should be headed by Professor / Director / Head of the University Department as per the nomenclature in the University for the same position with major responsibilities similar to that of the head of any other teaching department.

9.3 The University, in accordance with the status of the Department, shall give academic freedom to this Department for the planning and conduct of innovative programmes in Teaching, Research, Extension and Field Outreach.

9.4 The faculty of the Department is also eligible for the Unassigned Grant of the UGC available to the university and for the research and other grants of the various UGC schemes for teachers.

9.5 Departments already in existence shall be eligible for Special Assistance Programs (SAP) and other such special assistance schemes of the UGC and other national / international agencies

(B) Nomenclature of the Departments

Those Departments which are already known as Departments of Adult, Continuing Education and Extension or any other name approved by the university, may retain the nomenclature. In case of new Departments, they should adopt the nomenclature Departments of Adult, Continuing Education and Extension and Field Outreach (ACEEFO). For the purpose of these guidelines the Departments are referred to as Departments of Adult, Continuing Education, Extension and Field Outreach (ACEE & FO).

(C) Structure

1. At the UGC level

The Commission may constitute Expert Committee(s) to examine proposals from universities for financial support under the scheme for fresh induction, advice on policy matters, monitor and review of the Departments completing its tenure, implementation and utilization. The Committee will also be responsible for finalizing consolidated activity wise and program wise annual and action plan for the X Plan, reviewing performance reports from the Departments for further action.

2. At the University level

(i) Advisory Committee

Since the university is the focus of continuing and extension education and outreach activities, it is necessary to have an Advisory Committee of Adult and Continuing Education and Extension and Field Outreach to oversee various academic and extension field outreach programmes of the university. The Advisory Committee will have members as representatives from (a) the Syndicate / Executive Council / Management Council, (b) UGC representative from the concerned Bureau, (c) representative of NLMA/SLMA, (d) Heads of University Departments / Principals (for Colleges) in concerned areas, (e) two three experts in the field, (f) Government Departments and (g) NGOs. The membership of the committee may be from 10-12. The Head of Department of Adult and Continuing Education and Extension and Field Outreach will be its Member-Secretary. The Advisory Committee must meet at least twice a year, advise and take steps on courses, curriculum, prepare the annual programme of activity ties, look into proper utilization of grants, monitor and review the implementation of the programme with the help of Implementation Committee.

(ii) Implementation Committee

In order to facilitate the functioning of the Department, an Implementation Committee, consisting of 4/6 members of the Advisory Committee including 1/2 local members in the areas may be constituted with the Director as the Convener The Implementation Committee must meet once in 2 to : months. This Committee may also recommend introducing certificate and other short-term courses, suggesting course guest faculty, determining eligibility of students, lay down fee structure and evaluating the programmes.

(iii) The Board

To advise the Department in academic matters including research in the area of ACEE and FO and monitor academic activities, an Academic Board will be constituted as per the university procedure in the form of a Regular Board of Studies

(D) Faculty and Staff

1. Head / Director of the Department of Adult Continuing Education, Extension Education and Field Outreach

Each Department will have a Head/Director. The Department will be headed by a Professor / Director, directly responsible to the Vice-Chancellor to whom he / she will report. The Professor / Director of the Department may be selected on part time basis from the disciplines/department of Adult Education / Social Sciences / Education / Humanities / Management with experience in teaching, research, extension work and field outreach.

The duties of the Professor / Director will be similar to those of Heads of other teaching departments. However, he/ she will have the additional responsibility of implementing the UGC guidelines for the scheme. Since extension has to be the focus of the university, the Professor/ Director of the Department should possess considerable leadership qualities in continuing and extension education, field outreach programmes.

2. Faculty

The faculty for the Department of Adult and Continuing Education may be engaged on contract basis or on per lecture basis as per the rates approved by the Commission. All these appointments are within the approved budget.

3. Secretarial and Non-teaching Technical Staff

The Department will have Secretarial and Non-teaching Technical Staff whose service conditions shall be the same as are applicable to other non-academic staff of the university and they will be eligible to all benefits like pension/CPG/GPF, medical aid, etc.

4. Field Investigator/Project Assistant

In the Tenth Plan period the Department will be permitted to appoint from the salary component of the UGC grant, additional manpower of 3 to 5 Field Investigators/Project Assistants to implement its programs.

(i) Qualifications and Experience

(a) Graduates or Post Graduates with at least one year's office/ field experience in Adult and Continuing Education and Extension and not more than 35 years of age and

(b) Graduates/Post Graduates with a diploma in Adult and Continuing Education & Extension and related fields will be given preference. However, the age of such candidates will not be more than 35 years.

(ii) Selection Procedure and Appointment

The advertisement, selection and appointment shall be made by the Department itself after obtaining the University permission. The appointment shall be on a contract basis for the Tenth Plan period only. The candidate will have no claim or right for re-appointment or permanency;

(iii) Role and Functions

The Field Investigator/Project Assistant shall carry out academic, administrative and supporting field activities as directed by the Head/Director of the Department

(iv) Compensation/Salary

Field Investigator/Project Assistant shall be entitled to a consolidated amount of

(a) Graduate - minimum of Rs. 4000/- per month and Rs. 500/- Fixed Travel Allowance and

(b) Post-Graduate ? minimum of Rs. 6000/- per month and Rs. 500/- Fixed Travel Allowance.

(v) Supervision

His/Her work will be supervised/monitored by the Head/ Director of the Department.

5. Project staff on hiring

No regular or contract staff is permissible under the scheme other than mentioned above. The miscellaneous work of the Department may be got done by outsourcing on hiring basis.

10. Nodal Universities

The UGC has identified Nodal Universities and also defined their service areas. The Nodal University is a link between the UGC and the universities in the service area. During the Tenth Plan the Nodal Agency System will be continued. However, the Nodal Agencies will be reviewed in the Tenth Plan by the UGC Committee of Experts. New Nodal Agencies may also be considered based on the performance and requirements In addition to the normal responsibilities expected of a Department, each University, being a nodal University, will have the following functions and roles:

(A) Co-coordinating role —

- New initiatives, specially in designing courses;

- Disseminating information on innovative programs and

- Motivating universities in the service area for strengthening the programme by organizing orientation / training programs.

(B) Documentation and Dissemination of information—

- Documentation ? Building Archives;
- Updated reference lists of available material for dissemination ? Books, Journals and Audio-visual materials;
- Use of new technology like Internet, Publishing Newsletter, creating websites and
- Publications

(C) Networking at different levels with —

- Government programmes;
- Ministries connected with outreach work;
- Official bodies;
- Other universities, professional bodies / training centres and
- Non-governmental Organizations and their networks, Civil Societies

(D) Advocacy—

Liasioning with UGC, State Government, Vice-Chancellors? Committees, State Council for Higher Education, Universities, drawing attention to critical issues;

Each Nodal University will convene two meetings of the Departments in its Service Area every year. The meetings are conducted at different universities in the service area by rotation. At least, at one of the meetings every year, a UGC officer is invited for interaction, who should report his / her observations to the UGC Committee of Experts. The departments will be responsible for submitting the annual report and review proforma to their respective Nodal Agency. The Nodal Agency shall be responsible for preparing a comprehensive report of the Departments in its service area and submit the same to UGC;

The UGC shall convene a meeting of the Directors of Nodal Agencies, at least once a year and The Nodal University is expected to be dynamic, rather than routine, if it must fulfill its role and responsibility effectively. For this p purpose, the Nodal University must prepare an annual work plan through which it can appraise its performance.

11. Administrative and Financial Procedures

11.1 Re-appropriation within the budget heads upto 10 percent will be permitted by the UGC with the approval of Vice-Chancellor. If more re-appropriation is needed, the prior approval of the UGC will have to be sought.

11.2 Non-recurring grants are for a period of five years whereas annual recurring grants are for the particular year for which it has been sanctioned

12. Funding Criteria and Pattern of Assistance

12.1 It is proposed that every university should set up a Department of ACEE & FO. To begin with in the Tenth Plan, the number of Departments of ACEE & FO would be increased;

12.2 Financial support is given in a flexible manner for an earmarked group of activities;

12.3 In order to give flexibility to the utilization of grants, the grants will be permitted to be carried forward from year to year till the end of the Plan period. However, these grants will be accountable within the grant norms;

12.4 UGC may categorize the Departments based on review by the expert committee;

12.5 In order to give greater stability to the Departments, the salary and benefits for the core staff shall be included in the comprehensive annual budget of the university and in the total Plan proposals of the concerned universities;

12.6 UGC's support for the establishment of a new Department will be till the end of X Plan Period;

12.7 The State Universities will have to obtain the State Government's concurrence to give permanency to the posts created for permanent positions, especially under earlier plans, if not done already. The University/State Government must take suitable steps.

The State Government's concurrence will also be required for the core faculty sanctioned for a new Department;

12.8 As far as new Departments are concerned, the post of one Reader and one Lecturer will be sanctioned in addition to the provision of grants under the salary component. It will be the responsibility of the concerned University to provide non-teaching administrative/ office staff, accommodation, furniture and other infrastructure facilities;

12.9 The Department will need to explore other sources for raising funds in addition to the UGC assistance;

12.10 Conducting self-financing programmes / courses is essential for the sustainability of the Department;

12.11 A separate fund is created from the resources generated by the Department, to be utilized for the activities of the Department;

12.12 A separate budget is maintained for the Department operating with the UGC and State Government grants;

12.13. The Department may establish

(i) Student Counseling / Placement / Career Guidance Centre;

(ii) e - Learning Centre in Departments which submit a specific proposal for the same. About 30 Centres of each type will be set up in the Tenth Plan Period. The one-time grant for the Plan Period for these Centres will be as given below:-

(a) Student Counseling / Placement /Career Guidance Centre - Rs. 2,25,000

(b) e-Learning Center, development of website, e-learning packages, on? line courses, etc. - Rs. 6,00,000

12.14. Grants for the Nodal Agency - Rs. 75,000 per annum

12.15. In order to be eligible to the grants for the Tenth Plan, each University will have to submit a certificate signed by the Vice-Chancellor, accepting the Tenth Plan Guidelines.

Appendix – II

Checklists and Interview Schedule utilized in the study

(i) Checklist to assess the relevance of Adult Education Programme

1. Adult Education Programme will be helpful to eradicate illiteracy from the region.

2. Adult Education Programme will help in removing poverty from the region.

3. Adult Education Programme will help reduce population growth in the region.

4. Adult Education Programme will be helpful towards developing social, economic and political consciousness.

5. Adult Education Programme will be helpful in putting an end to social ill-traditions prevalent in the region.

6. Adult Education Programme will strengthen environmental protection and enrichment.

7. Adult Education Programme will nurture religious tolerance among the people in the region.

8. Adult Education Programme will help foster national integration in the region.

9. Adult Education Programme will help in developing small and agriculture industries in the region.

10. Adult Education Programme will generate awareness regarding entitlements available to the people under the various development programmes.

11. Adult Education Programme will raise levels of vocational proficiency among the adults in the region.

12. Adult Education Programme will help generate greater interest among the people in the region in the awareness being nurtured by the communication media.

13. Adult Education Programme will raise levels of health awareness among the people in the region.

14. Adult Education Programme will encourage people to seek participation in education programmes through correspondence courses and distance education programmes.

15. Adult Education Programme will enable people to collectively fight instances of social injustice.

16. Adult Education Programme will encourage correct use of fertilizers, soil testing and high yielding varieties of seeds.

17. Adult Education Programme will foster a better sense of budgeting resources available to the adults at home.

18. Adult Education Programme will generate awareness concerning foods and nutrition.

(ii) Checklist for suggestions in regard to the greater effectiveness of the Programme

1. Awareness among people towards Adult Education Programme is developed.

2. Various cultural programmes are linked with this programme and related assistance be provided.

3. Adult Education Programme with economic programmes is linked.

4. Neo-literates for self-employment are encouraged.

5. Neo-literates are provided with the benefits of TRYSEM and IRDP schemes.

6. Each student of College/University should make at least 5 persons literate.

7. Adult Education is included as a subject of study at the undergraduate level.

8. Proper environment should be built before starting the Programme.

9. Adult Education workers should be given training at the proper time.

10. Teaching-learning material should be made available right from the beginning.

11. Village Level Committees are formed to review the progress of Adult Education activities from time to time.

12. Persons engaged in different occupations are encouraged to participate in the programme through special subsidies and incentives.

(iii) Checklist related with the benefits accruing from the Programme

1. Adult Education Programme develops mutual cooperation among the learners.

2. Adult Education Programme promotes national integration.
3. Adult Education Programme familiarizes the learners with the small family norm.
4. Adult Education Programme develops awareness concerning the need for cleanliness.
5. The Adult learner spends his/her daily life in an organized manner.
6. The Adult learner helps women to keep their homes neat and clean.
7. Adult Education Programme makes the learners understand the importance of plantation.
8. Adult Education Programme creates awareness concerning the small savings schemes.
9. Adult Education Programme raises awareness about preventive health care.
10. Adult Education Programme raises knowledge about food grains storage and protection.
11. Adult Education Programme raises knowledge about resources available under the various programmes of the Government.
12. Adult Education Programme raises awareness about the principles of General Science.
13. Adult Education Programme raises awareness about laws affecting the lives of citizens.
14. Adult Education Programme acquaints the learners with the basic tenets of each religion.

15. Adult Education Programme raises awareness about the national festivals.

16. Adult Education Programme enhances political awareness.

17. Adult Education Programme enhances social awareness.

18. Adult Education Programme equips learners to fight against social evils.

19. Adult Education Programme promotes self-dependence among the learners.

20. Adult Education Programme acquaints the learners with their cultural heritage.

(iv) Checklist regarding benefits accruing from Functionality

1. Adult Education Programme enhances the learner's occupational skills.

2. Adult Education Programme sharpens the farming skills of the learners.

3. Adult Education Programmes acquaints the learners with the high yielding varieties in agriculture.

4. Adult Education Programme acquaints the learners with the ways to eradicate plant diseases.

5. Adult Education Programme promotes knowledge concerning the use of fertilizers.

6. Adult Education Programme promotes skills in cottage industries like Poultry, Fishery, Piggery, etc.

7. Women learners acquire skills in and income from embroidery, knitting, sewing, painting, etc.

8. Women learners learn to utilize their leisure time in maintaining their homes neat and tidy.

9. Neo-literates become familiar with the importance of fruit-giving trees.

10. Learners can acquire skills and earn income from making dolls, wax and other items.

11. Learners can acquire skills in kitchen-gardening.

12. Learners can choose food full of proteins and vitamins.

13. Learners can acquire knowledge of and skills in fuel saving.

(v) Checklist concerning benefits accruing from Literacy

1. The neo-literates acquire knowledge of alphabets.

2. The learners slowly start making words and sentences.

3. The learners are able to read and write gradually.

4. The learners can read the headlines of the newspapers.

5. The learners can gradually learn to read religious books.

6. The learners can use mathematics in their daily life.

7. The learners can read advertisements concerning government policies and programmes.

8. The learners can fight the crooks and cheats.

9. The learners can handle documents related to their land and other property.

10. The learners can buy their bus and rail tickets without any body's help.

11. The learners can confidently ask for loans from banks for their business.

12. The learners can manage their own home budget.

(vi) Interview Schedule for various functionaries in the Programme

1. Was there proper environment building for the Programme in your village?

2. Did you participate in the Survey or in environment building?

3. Has any Kala Jatha, Paidal Jatha or Vigyan Jatha visited your area?

4. In your opinion, did environment building generate motivation for Adult Education among the village population?

5. Were you selected on a voluntary basis?

6. Have you received training for the work?

7. Were you given adequate learning materials during the training?

8. Were you satisfied with the training?

9. Did you try to teach all the ten illiterates that came in contact with you?

10. What were the difficulties faced by you during your work?

    (a) shortage of teaching-learning material

    (b) improper lighting at the place of learning

    (c) lack of interest among the learners

    (d) shortage of time

11. Where did you carry on your teaching-learning work?
    (a) school

    (b) home

12. How many days did you devote for teaching-learning work?
    (a) Less than one month

    (b) One to six months

    (c) More than six months

13. Were you able to complete teaching of the lessons in time?

14. Were you otherwise encouraged for this work?

15. Is there any Village Level Literacy Committee?

16. Did any Senior Officer visit your village/area to discuss your difficulties?

17. Which of the three measures would make this programme successful?
    a) arrangement of proper lighting

    b) remuneration for teaching

    timely distribution of teaching-learning materials

Appendix – III

Size of the Programme at the University of Gorakhpur

Year	*No. of Centres Organized*	*No. of persons enrolled*	*No. of persons made literate*
1979-80	170	5134	4710
1980-81	140	4094	3678
1981-82	150	4436	4133
1982-83	130	3923	3550
1983-84	1040	30955	26544
1984-85	980	29232	26489
1985-86	1020	30491	26849
1986-87	970	28880	25540
1987-88	970	28735	25625
1988-89	420	12583	9941
1989-90	360	10783	8269
1990-91	360	9576	6879
1991-92	360	9600	6825

Bibliography

Adiseshiah, Malcolm S. Adult Education Faces Inequalities. Madras: Sangam Publishers, 1981.

—————————. Functionalities of Literacy Campaign are a Turning Point for Literacy. (ed.) Leon Bataille. Oxford: Revgaman Press, 1981.

Aggarwal, Binod C. Higher Education through Television: The Indian Experience. New Delhi: Concept Publishing Co., 2000.

Aggarwal, SP. Development of Adult and Non-Formal Education in India. New Delhi: Concept Publishing Co. 2002.

Agnihotri, S. Evaluation of the programme of Adult Education in operation under the Pilot Plan in Wardha District. Nagpur: Doctoral Dissertation, Nagpur University, 1974.

Akhtar, Naseem H. A study of the Non-Formal Educational (NFE) Needs of the Muslim Women in the City of Madras and Developing An Appropriate NFE Curriculum Design. Madras: Doctoral Dissertation, University of Madras, 1987.

Altbach, Philip G. Higher Education in the Third World: Themes and Variations. New Delhi: Radiant, 1990.

Ansari, NA. An appraisal of the training programmes for Social Education Workers in India. Delhi: Doctoral Dissertation, University of Delhi, 1969.

——————. Adult Education in India. New Delhi: S. Chand & Co., 1990.

Athreya, Venkatesh B. and Chunkath, Sheela Rani. Literacy and empowerment. New Delhi: Sage Publications, 1996.

Ausubel, DP. The Psychology of Meaningful Verbal Learning. New York: Grune and Stratton, 1963.

Balasaravanan, T. Study of Attitude and Achievement of Women Neo-Literates of Post Literacy Programmes under NLM in Pudukkottai District, Tamil Nadu. Tiruchirappalli: Doctoral Dissertation, Bharathidasan University, 1996.

Bertelsen, PH. "Adult Education: A position paper". UNESCO: Report, 1974.

Bhagria, Rita. The impact of polyvalent education of Shramik Vidyapeeths on the Industrial Workers. Chandigarh: Doctoral Dissertation, Punjab University, 1992.

Bhatia, SC. And Srivastava, RN. Literacy, Literacy Materials and their Preparation: A General Perspective. New Delhi: Directorate of Adult Education, Ministry of Education, 1978.

Bhatia, SC and Patil, BR. Research in Adult Education. New Delhi: Indian Adult Education Association, 1983.

Bhatia, SC (ed.). Some Critical Considerations in Adult Education. Delhi: University of Delhi, 1980.

————— (ed.) Children in India. Delhi: Indian University Association for Continuing Education, 1990.

Bhatia, SC. Education and Socio-Cultural Disadvantage. Delhi: Xerxes Publications, 1982.

—————. "An Area Development Approach in Extension". IUACE News, Vol. 8, 2, March-April, 1987.

—————. Education for SC/ST: Utilization Patterns. New Delhi: Development Communication Services, 1992.

—————. Universal Literacy By Fits and Starts. New Delhi: Monitoring and Documentation Services, 1996.

Bhandari, JS. Factors affecting persistency and dropout of Adult Literacy classes in Udaipur District. Udaipur: Doctoral Dissertation, Agricultural University, 1974.

Bharat Gyan Vigyan Samithi. A Guide Book for Mass Campaign for Total Literacy. New Delhi: BGVS, 1992.

Bhatt, Suman Seva. A study of growth and development of Adult Education Programmes in India. Kurukshetra: Doctoral Dissertation, University of Kurukshetra, 1990.

Bhola, HS. Evaluation of Functional Literacy. Tehran: Hulton Educational Publication Ltd. In co-operation with the International Institute for Adult Literacy Methods, Tehran, 1979.

—————. World Trends and Issues in Adult Education. Paris: UNESCO, 1988.

—————. Campaigning for Literacy. Paris: UNESCO, 1984.

Bhushan, A. Encyclopedia of Adult Education and Literacy. New Delhi: Anmol Publications Pvt. Ltd., 2005.

Bordia, Anil. Farmers Training and Functional Literacy. New Delhi: Indian Adult Education Association, 1975.

Bourman and Anderson. Literacy and Economic Development.: The American Higher Education. San Francisco: Josse4y-Boss Publishers, 1978.

Brockmeier, Jens, Wang, Min, and Olson, David R (eds.). Literacy, Narrative and Culture. Richmond, UK. Curzon Press, 2002.

Brundage, DH. Adult Learning Principles and their application to Program Planning. Toronto: Ontario Institute for Studies in Education, 1980.

Chandel, NPS. A cost-effectiveness analysis of the National Adult Education Programme with special reference to the Seventh Five Year Plan. Agra: Doctoral Dissertation, Dayalbagh Educational Institute, 1992.

Chandrasekar, Rajkumari. Aspects of Adult Education. Madras: New Era Publications, 1982.

Chaturvedi, SC. Impact of Social Education on the life and the living of the people in Block Areas in the District of Gorakhpur, Jhansi, Lucknow and Mathura. Lucknow: Doctoral Dissertation, Department of Social Work, University of Lucknow, 1969.

Chaube, M. Youth Welfare Programme in India with special reference to Uttar Pradesh. Lucknow: Doctoral Dissertation, University of Lucknow, 1963.

Chitra, M. A Study of Perception and Attitude of Learners at Selected Functional Literacy Centres in Tamil Nadu with regard to Developmental Messages Delivered through Distance Education Technology of Audio Forum. Madras: Doctoral Dissertation, University of Madras, 1992.

Chugani, R. A study of Rural Functional Literacy Project in North Arcot District of Tamil Nadu. Vadodara: Doctoral Dissertation, The Maharaja Sayajirao University of Baroda, 1987.

Coles, ET. Adult Education in Developing Countries. Oxford: Pergamon Press, 1977.

Coombs, Philip. New Paths to Learning. Paris: UNICEF/ICED, 1973.

Coombs, Philip and Manzoor, A. Attacing Rural Poverty – How Non-formal Education can help. Baltimore: John Hopkins University, 1974.

Correa, Lawrence. Adult Education for Social Development with Special Reference to Andhra Pradesh. New Delhi: Himalaya Publishing House, 1995.

Das, Manoranjan. A study of the socio-economic problems in the implementation of the Adult Education Programme in Assam. Guwahati: Gauhati University, 1990.

Daswani, CJ. Adult Education in India: Selected Papers. New Delhi: UNESCO, 2000.

Dave, RH. The Report of the Committee on Evaluation of Total Literacy Campaign and Declaration of Learning Outcomes. New Delhi: MHRD, 1992.

Dave, RH and Perera, DA. Learning Strategies for Post-Literacy and Continuing Education: A Cross-National Perspective. Hamburg: UIE, 1988.

Degenae, Alain and Forse, Michel (eds.). Introducing Social Networks. London: Sage Publications, 1999.

Desai, DB, Yadav, MS, Govinda, R. and Lakshmi, TKS. Evaluation of the National Adult Education Programme in Seven Districts of Gujarat – 19780-1980. Vadodara: The Maharaja sayjirao University of Baroda, 1982.

Dhababal, KR. Impact of Rural Functional components on Adult Literates in Sakkottai Block. Karaikudi: M. Phil Dissertation, Alagappa University, 1991.

Deshpande, BS. Informal Education through the Saints Literature of the Middle Ages in Marathi. Poona: Doctoral Dissertation, University of Poona, 1975.

Dixit, Asha. A study of educational need pattern of adults in the Urban, Rural and Tribal Communities of Rajasthan. Jaipur: Doctoral Dissertation, University of Rajasthan, 1975.

Dixit, AP. Non-Formal & Continuing Education. New Delhi: Vista International Publishing House, 2005.

Draper, James A. Adult Education: A Focus for the Social Sciences. New Delhi: Industrial Law Advisory Services, 1989.

Dreze, Jean and Sen, Amartya (eds.). Indian Development: Selected Regional Perspectives. New Delhi: Oxford University Press, 1997.

——————————————. India: Development and Participation. New Delhi: Oxford University Press, 2002./

Dreze, Jean and Gazdar, Harris. "Uttar Pradesh: The Burden of Inertia", in Jean Dreze and Amartya Sen (eds.). op. cit.

Dubashi, PR. "New Remedies for Poverty", Part I and II. New Delhi: Financial Express, June 29 and 30, 1983.

Dutta, SC. History of Adult Education in India. New Delhi: Industrial Law Advisory Servicie, 1986.

Elias, M. A Study of Psycho-Social Correlates of Adult Learning and Development in Selected Literacy centres in Chengai-Anna District of Tamil Nadu. Madras: Doctoral Dissertation, University of Madras, 1991.

Gadgil, DR. Investigation into the problem of lapse into Illiteracy in the Satara District. Poona: Gokhale Institute of Politics and Economics, 1975.

Gandhian Institute of Studies. Voluntary Action for Adult Literacy. Varanasi: Gandhian Institute of Studies, 1969.

Gayatonde, NV. The problems of Social Education in India with special reference to Maharashtra, Gujarat, Rajasthan, Madhya Pradesh, Mysore, Karnataka. Poona: Doctoral Dissertation, University of Poona, 1977.

Gill, Kirrin. If We Walk Together – Communities, NGOs, and Government in Partnership for Health – The Hyderabad Experience. New Delhi: The World Bank, 1999.

Government of India, Ministry of Human Resource Development. Towards Enlightened and Humane Society. Report of the Committee for Review of National Policy on Education 1986. Department of Education, MHRD, Government of India, 1990.

——————————. The Turning Point: Some Thoughts on Adult Education. New Delhi: Directorate of Adult Education, MHRD, Government of India, 1992.

——————————. National Policy on Education 1986: Programme of Action 1992. New Delhi: Department of Education, MHRD, Government of India, 1992.

———————. Education for All: The Indian Scene. New Delhi: Department of Education, MHRD, Government of India, 1993.

———————. Evaluation of Literacy campaigns in India: Report of the Experts Group. New Delhi: Department of Education, MHRD, Government of India, 1994.

———————. Planning Commission. Report of the Steering Committee on Elementary and Adult Education for the Tenth Five Year Plan (2002-2007), December 2001.

———————. Department of Health and Family Welfare (2000). Uttar Pradesh Population Policy.

Government of Uttar Pradesh. Human Development Report 2003, Uttar Pradesh. Lucknow: Planning Department, Government of Uttar Pradesh, 2003.

Jacob, PJ. Identification of certain curricular areas in functional Science and construction of select models for Adult Education. Trivandrum: Doctoral Dissertation, University of Kerala, 1990.

Janardhana Rao, V. Problems of Continuing Education. New Delhi: Discovery Publishing House, 2005.

Jarvis, P. Adult and Continuing Education – Theory and Practice. London: Croom Helm, 1983.

Jayagopal. R. Village Case Studies in Literacy Programmes. Madras: University of Madras, 1981.

———————. Adult Learning – A Psycho-Social Analysis in the Indian Context; Madras: University of Madras, 1985.

__________. Human Resource Development: Conceptual Analysis and Strategies. New Delhi: Sterling Publishers Pvt. Ltd., 1990.

Jethithor, Bharat. Adult Education and Extension. New Delhi: APH Publishing Co., 1996.

Jeyapal, P. A Study of Jana Shikshan Nilayam (Post Literacy and Continuing Education Centre) under NLM with reference to Chingleput District of Tamil Nadu. Madras: Doctoral Dissertation, University of Madras, 1990.

Johnston, JP. A proposal for the establishment of a State-wide Adult Education Programme for Madras, Tamil Nadu. Madras: Doctoral Dissertation, University of Madras, 1970.

Kameshwaran, Janaki. Study of Selected Folk Arts and its Effectiveness in terms of chosen Dependent Variables on the Urban Adult Women Learners. Madras: Doctoral Dissertation, University of Madras, 1986.

Kapali, NVR. A Study of Environmental Perception of Rural Adults in Chingleput District of Tamil Nadu. Madras: Doctoral Dissertation, University of Madras, 1986.

Karlekar, Malavika. Paradigms of Learning: The Total Literacy Campaign in India. New Delhi: Sage Publications, 2004.

Karuppaiyan, S. A Study on Retention of Literacy among the Neo-Literates of Total Literacy Campaign in Puddukkottai District, Tamil Nadu. Tiruchirappalli: Doctoral Dissertation, Bharathidasan University, 1998.

Kaul, PN. Attitudes towards Extension Education of Undergraduate Agricultural students of the PAU at various stages in their Instruction. Ludhiana: Doctoral Dissertation, Punjab Agricultural University, 1970.

Kaur, Manjeet. Development of learning packages for illiterate adults of Punjab. Patiala: Doctoral Dissertation, Punjabi University, 1992.

Khajapeer, M. A study of the academic performance of the Farmers' Functional Literacy Programme participants in relation to some social-psychological factors. Tirupati: Sri Venkateswara University, 1978.

Khan, MZ. The problems of Social Adult Education in the four districts of Bombay-Karnataka, Dharwar: Doctoral Dissertation, Karnataka University, 1958.

Kudesia. UC. The role of Social Education in Rural Development of Madhya Pradesh. Sagar: Doctoral Dissertation, Sagar University, 1973.

Kidd, JR. How Adults Learn. New York: Association Press, 1974.

Koshy, TA, Roy, Prodipto, and Jesudasan, Victor. The Mahabubnagar Experiment Non-formal Education for Rural Women, New Delhi: Council for Social Development, 1976.

Knowles, S. Malcolm. The Modern Practice of adult Education: Andragogy versus Pedagogy. New York: Association Press, 1970.

————————. Adult Learner: A Neglected Species. London: Gulf Publishers, 1984.

Kumaraswamy, T. Total Literacy Campaign: Problems and Issues. New Delhi: Sonali Publications, 2005.

Kundu, CL. Adult Education: Principles, Practice and Prospects. New Delhi: Sterling Publishers Pvt. Ltd, 1984.

Liveright, AA and Haygood, N. (eds). The Exter Papers. Boston, 1969.

Mali, MG. Factors affecting retention of Literacy among Adult Neo-literates. Doctoral Dissertation, 1974.

Mallikarjuaswamy, M. Survey of reading needs and interests of Adult Neo-literates in Mysore State. Mysore: Mysore State Adult Education Council, 1969.

____________. Word list in Kannada for Neo-literates. Mysore: Mysore State Adult Education Council, 1969.

Manavalane, R. An evaluation of the Adult Education Programme implemented by the Annamalai University in the Keerappalayam Panchayat Union in Chidambaram Taluka. Annamalai Nagar: M. Phil Dissertation, Annamalai University, 1990.

Marshall, Judith. Literacy, State Formation and People's Power. Bellville: University of Western Cape, 1990.

Maslow, AM. Motivation and Personality. New York: Harper and Row, 1954.

Miller, HL. Teaching and learning in Adult Education. New York: The Macmillan Company, 1964.

Mishra, Lakshmidhar. Literacy and Human Development. New Delhi: National Literacy Mission, 1992.

Mohan, S. et al. Total Literacy Campaign – Pasumpon Muthuramalingam Thevar District – An Evaluation. Karaikudi: Department of Education, Alagappa University, 1993.

Mohan, Shantha N. and Usha, MN. Total literacy Campaign in Bijapur and Dakshina Kannada Districts in

Karnataka: An evaluation. Bangalore: an independent study, Institute for Social and EconomicChange, 1992.

Mohanty, BB. Adult Education: Some Reflections. New Delhi: Industrial Law Advisory Service, 1989.

Mohanty, JN. Adult and Non-Formal Education. New Delhi: Deep and Deep Publications, 1991.

Mohanty, Nibedita; Evaluation of the Functional Literacy Programme in Puri District in Orissa. Pune: Indian Institute of Education, 1988.

Murthy, Samba D. A study of the factors responsible for the effective implementation of the National Adult Education Programme in Andhra Pradesh. Hyderabad: Doctoral Dissertation, Osmania University, 1988.

Muthumanickam. A Study of Selected Rural Television Forums with Regard to Knowledge and Attitude Levels of the Adult Learners. Madras: Doctoral Dissertation, University of Madras, 1991.

Nagappa, TR. Survey of reading needs and interests of Adult Neo-literates in Mysore State. Mysore: Mysore State Adult Education Council, 1966.

Nanda, SK. A critical study of the Development of Adult Education in the Punjab during the period from 1947-1972. Patiala: Doctoral Dissertation, Punjabi University, 1978.

National Literacy Mission. Evaluation of Literacy Campaigns – Summary Reports. New Delhi: Directorate of Adult Education, MHRD, Government of India, 1995.

————————————. Status of Adult Literacy in India: A Database for Literacy Programmes. Compiled and explained by Prem Chand. New Delhi: Directorate of Adult Education, Ministry of Human Resource Development, 2007.

———————————. Recognition of Literacy Initiatives. New Delhi: Department of School Education & Literacy, Ministry of Human Resource Development, 2007.

———————————. Leading the Way: New Initiatives in Adult Education. (eds.) Vandana Kumari Jena and A. Mathew. New Delhi: Directorate of Adult Education, Department of School Education & Literacy, Ministry of Human Resource Development, 2008.

Nayak, AK. Life-Long and Continuing Education. Delhi: Indian Publishers Distributors, 1997.

Olson, David R. and Torrance, Nancy (eds.) The Making of Literate Societies. Massachussets, USA: Blackwell Publishers, 2001.

Padmini, N.A study of Arivoli Iyakkam Mass Literacy Programme in the selected areas of Pondicherry Region. Dindigul: M. Phil Dissertation. Avinashlingam Institute of Home Science and Higher Education for Women, 1992.

Pal, RS. A critical study of Farmer's Training and Education Programme in relation to the changes in their behavioural components. New Delhi: Doctoral Dissertation, Indian Agricultural Research Institute, 1970.

Pandian, M. Soundra. Literacy Campaign in India. New Delhi: Discovery Publishing House, 2000.

Pankajam, G. Extension: Third Dimension of Education. Delhi: Gian Publishing House, 2000.

Parashar, BP. A Textbook of Adult Education. New Delhi: Dominant Publishers and Distributors, 2005.

Parkash, Braham. The impact of Fuctional Literacy in the Rural Areas of Haryana and the Union Territory of Delhi. Kurukshetra: Doctoral Dissertation, University of Kurukshetra, 1978.

Parthasarathy, K. A Study of Persuasive Communication Techniques and its effect on Adult Learning at Selected Villages of Chingleput District in Tamil Nadu. Madras: Doctoral Dissertation, University of Madras, 1987.

———————. Adult Education Programme in Eight South East Asian Countries (Bangladesh, Pakistan, Nepal, Burma, China, Thailand, Sri Lanka and Indonesia. Madras: State Resource Centre, 1988.

———————. Rural Development Programmes in India with reference to Five Year Plans, Lifelong learning for Social Development. The Netherlands: The University of Nijmegen, 2002.

———————. Experiments in Community Empowerment. Tiruchirappalli: Bharathidasan University, 2006.

———————. Facets of Adult and Continuing Education. Tiruchirappalli: Bharathidasan University, 2006.

Patel, RBA. A critical survey of Social Education in the State of Gujarat. Doctoral Dissertation, Sardar Patel University, 1970.

Pathak, SN. Adult education and socio-economic development of Azamgarh District. Lucknow: independent study, Govind Vallabh Pant Institute of Studies in Rural Development, 1991.

Pillai, Sivadasan. Trends and Problems in Adult Education. Ambala: Associate Publishers, 1990.

Prasad, H. Literacy and Development. Varanasi: Regional Planning Wing, Gandhian Institute of Studies, 1967.

Prasad, R. Adult Education. New Delhi: Ashish Publishing House, 1991.

Public Report on Basic Education in India. New Delhi: Oxford University Press, 1999.

Rajan, R. A critical study of Mass Programme of Functional Literacy in Tamil Nadu. Pune: Indian Institute of Education, 1992.

__________. Adult Education by NSS Volunteers. Chennai: Sangeetha Publications, 1998.

Ramabrahman, I. Adult Education Policy and Performance. New Delhi: Ayan Publishing House, 2005.

Ramadevi, B. A comparative study of the organization and conduct of various agencies involved in the Adult Education Programmes in Kerala. Trivandrum: Doctoral Dissertation, University of Kerala, 1990.

Ramanna, R. Literacy in India. New Delhi: Indian Publishers Distributors, 2001.

Rao, GS Literacy Survey of the Class-IV Employees of the University of Mysore. Mysore: Central Institute of Indian Languages, 1974.

Rashid, Abdur. An Enquiry into the problem of motivation for Adult Literacy. Delhi: Jamia Millia Islamia, 1966.

Rathnayya, EV. Structural Constraints in Tribal Education: A Regional Study. Udaipur: Doctoral Dissertation, Department of Sociology, University of Udaipur, 1974.

Reddy, Adinarayana P. A study of certain socio-psychological factors relating to the Adult Education Instructor effectiveness. Tirupati: Doctoral Dissertation, Sri Venkateswara University, 1990.

——————. Adult Education Programmes in India. Allahabad: Chugh Publications, 1990.

——————. Determinants of Adult Education Instructor effectiveness: Independent Study. Tirupati: Sri Venkateswara University, 1992.

——————. Literacy and Development. Delhi: Discovery Publishing House, 2005.

—————— (ed.). Literacy for Globalization. Ambala: Associated Publishers, 2007.

Reddy, GK, et al. Evaluation of Literacy Campaign in Visakapattinam District. Visakapattinam: Andhra University, 1993.

Reddy, Janardhana D. A study of certain factors related to persisters and drop-outs of Adult Education Centres. Tirupati: Doctoral Dissertation, Department of Education, Sri Venkateswara University, 1991.

Reddy, G. Lokanadha. Role Performance of Continuing Education Workers. New Delhi: Discovery Publishing House, 2000.

Reddy, Reddappa MC. Spatial variations of literacy in Andhra Pradesh. Tirupati: Doctoral Dissertation, Sri Venkateswara University, 1988.

Reddy, Subba PV. A study of job satisfaction of adult education supervisors in Andhra Pradesh. Tirupati: Doctoral

Dissertation, Department of Education, Sri Venkateswara University, 1991.

Reddy, V. Easwara. Education for All: The Knowledge Communication Mission. Hyderabad: AP State Advocacy Forum for Education for All, 1994.

Report of the National Seminar on National Policy on Education. Lagos: 1973.

Sachchidananda, and Sinha, AK. Evaluation of the Project on Radio Education for Adult Literacy. Independent Study. Patna: AN Sinha Institute of Social Studies, 1991.

Salamatullah. Adult Education Research in India: A Study. New Delhi: Industrial Law Advisory service, 1984.

Saldanha, D. The Literacy Campaign in Wardha District: A study of the programme for the age group 15-35 years. Independent Study. Bombay: Tata Institute of Social Sciences, 1992.

———. The Total Literacy Campaign in Sindhudurg District: A consolidated report. Independent Study. Bombay: Tata Institute of Social Sciences, 1992.

——— and Velaskar, Padma. Institutions of Higher Education and Extension: The case of Adult Education. Independent study. Bombay: Tata Institute of Social Sciences, 1991.

Saxena, JC National Literacy Mission: Problems and Prospects. New Delhi: Industrial Law Advisory Service, 1989.

Schenk, Hans (ed.). Living in India's Slums: A Case Study of Bangalore. Indo-Dutch Project on Alternatives in Development. New Delhi: Manohar Publications, 2001.

Sen, Amartya. Development as Freedom. New Delhi: Oxford University Press, 2000.

Seetharamu. AS and Ushadevi, MD. Adult Education in Karnataka State. Independent Study. Bangalore: Institute for Social and Economic Change, 1991.

Seetharamu, AD. Literacy Campaigns in India. New Delhi: Ashish Publishing House, 1997.

Shah, SY. Adult Education in Bihar. New Delhi: Commonwealth Publishers, 1989.

————————. A Source Book on Adult Education. New Delhi: Directorate of Adult Education, MHRD, Government of India, 1989.

Shanker, R. An Experiment in Functional Literacy Teaching through Naya Savera Method. Lucknow: Literacy House, 1972.

Sharma, B. Role Adult Education in Socio-Economic Development of Weaker Sections in Rural Areas of Uttar Pradesh: A Case Study of Rural Areas of Allahabad District. Independent Study. Allahabad: Indian Institute of Development Studies and Research, 1990.

Sharma, RD. "Theoretical approaches to Adult Learning". Indian Educational Review, Vol. 24, 4, pp. 47-9.

Shinde, PS. Communication patterns in Extension Education. Jaipur: Rawat Publications, 1997.

Shrivastava, Om. "Language Issue in Adult Education". Indian Journal of Adult Education, July 1980, p. 34.

Singh, BQ. The communication of ideas through Adult Education in India. Doctoral Dissertation, 1957.

Singh, DR. Studies in Adult and Non-Formal Education. New Delhi: Commonwealth Publishers, 2001.

Singh, Mubarak. Adult Education in India – Some Reflections. New Delhi: Kanishka Publishers and Distributors, 2004.

Singh, PP, and Shrma, S. Continuing Education Programme: Management and Implementation. New Delhi: Deep and Deep Publications, 2005.

Singh, UK. Life-Long Education. New Delhi: Commonwealth Publishers, 1997.

Sisodia, Yatindra Singh. Girls Literacy in Rural India: Comparative Study of Maharashtra and Madhya Pradesh. New Delhi: Rawat Publications, 2003.

Sivapalan, Unnithan TR. An enquiry into the Workers' Education Programme in Kerala with a view to suggest improvements. Trivandrum: Doctoral Dissertation, University of Kerala, 1991.

Srivastava, LRN. Development needs of the Tribal people. New Delhi: Tribal Education Unit, NCERT, 1970.

Surendra, G. Perspectives of Continuing Education Programme. New Delhi: Sonali Publications, 2005.

Talukdar, BK. Adult Education in Assam during the post-Independence period. Gauhati: Doctoral Dissertation, Department of Education, Gauhati University, 1975,

Tantray, GN. Adult Education in Jammu and Kashmir: An Appraisal. Srinagar: Doctoral Dissertation, University of Kashmir, 1990.

Thakre, PG. A study of the Adult Education Programme launched by Nagpur University and its impact on the target group. Nagpur: Doctoral Dissertation, Department of Education, Nagpur University, 1991.

Thandavakumari. Knowledge, Attitude and Practice of Rural and Urban Mothers on Child Nutrition. Tiruchirappalli: Doctoral Dissertation, Bharathidasan University, 2002.

The Mahbub ul Haq Development Centre. Human Development in South Asia 1999: The Crisis of Governance. Oxford: Oxford University Press, 1999.

Thomas, H. Briggs, Joseph, and Justman, J. Improving instruction through supervisor. New York: The MacMillan Company, 1952.

Thorndike, EL. Adult Learning. New York: Macmillan, 1928.

Triebel, Armin. "The Role of Literary Practices in the Activities and Institutions of Developed and Developing Countries", in Olson and Torrance (2001) op.cit.

Trivedi, RS. A critical survey of Social Education Programmes and Procedures in Kaira District. Vallab Vidyanagar: MB Patel College of Education, 1966.

Umayalparvathi, S. A Study of achievement, Motivation, Intelligence and Literacy Attainment in Some of the Urban and Rural Women Literacy Centres in Tamil Nadu and Pondicherry States. Madras: Doctoral Dissertation, University of Madras, 1982.

UNESCO. Draft Recommendations on the Development of Adult Education. Paris: UNESCO, 1976.

————————. The Hamburg Declaration and the Agenda for the Future. Hamburg: Fifth International Conference on Adult Education, 1977.

————. Asia Pacific Programme on Education for All (APPEAL). Bangkok: UNESCO Regional Office for Education in Asia and Pacific, 1986.

University Grants Commission. Development of Higher Education: A Policy Frame. New Delhi: University Grants Commission, 1978.

————. Report of the UGC Working Group on Point No. 16 of the New 20-Point Programme of the Government of India. New Delhi: University Grants Commission, 1983.

————. University System and Extension as the Third Dimension, Report of the Review Committee. New Delhi: University Grants Commission, 1987.

————. Consolidating the Past, Strengthening the Future. New Delhi: University Grants Commission, 2004.

Upasani, NK. Rural Enrichment Education Project featuring development of alternative models and strategies for self-learning for the rural youth on topics relevant to their life. Independent study. Pune: Adarsha Comprehensive College of Education and Research. 1988.

Uttar Pradesh Development Report, Vols. I & II. New Delhi: Academic Foundation, 2007. Prepared by Planning Commission, Government of India.

Varghese, Susan. Evaluation of teaching-learning materials in Malayalam used in Adult Education Centres in Kerala. Trivandrum: Doctoral Dissertation, Department of Education, University of Kerala, 1989.

Verma, Gita Dewan. Slumming India: A Chronicle of Slums and their Saviours. Penguin Books, 2002.

Verma, KK and Verma, Rajan. Evaluation of PREAL through holistic study: A study of village Gomti in Vaishali District of Bihar. Independent Study. Patna: AN Sinha Institute of Social Studies, 1992.

Vir, Dharam. A Study of Leisure time interests of Hindi-speaking villages from Psychology and Education Methods. International Alliance, 1968.

Vohra, Amarjit Singh. A Brief Report on Literacy and Post-Literacy Campaigns in India. New Delhi: National Literacy Mission, 1995.

Wadhwa, Shalini. Theory and Principles of Adult Education. New Delhi: Sarup Publications, 2000.

World Bank. India: Confronting Poverty: The Challenge of Uttar Pradesh (Draft). PREM: South Asia Region, 2001.

Index

A

Academic Community
  sensitization, 86-87
Academic Credit, 157
Access to resource urban areas,
  142
Adoption of village cluster,
  urban settlement, 102
Administration and Financial
  Procedures, 166
Adult Education Programme
  Relevance assessment
  checklist, 169 .
  Suggestions checklist, 169-
  170
  benefit accruing from
  –programme checklist, 171
  –functionaries checklist,
  173
  literacy checklist, 174
Advisory Committee of Adult
  and Continuing Education
  and Extension Field Out
  reach, 166
Advocacy for pro-poor rights,
  136,138
Adult literacy Campaigns
  responsê, 125
Adult Education
  meaning, 117-118
  definition issues raised, 92
  concepts, 19
  challenges,92
  gains from, 31
Agnihotri (1974), 33
Agriculture extension/
  diversification, 127
Agricultural Sector, 140
Andragogy, 20
  meaning, 22
  steps in (7), 22
  learning, 22-23
Andhra Pradesh, 33
Area Development Approach in
  Literacy and Adult
  Education, 43
Arts and Science Colleges, 85-86
Areas of Teaching chosen by
  universities, 98

Assam status, 33
Associate Degree/Diploma in Continuing Education, 155
Awareness component of NAEP, 42
Azamgarh District
  Adult Education, 68
  Socio-Economic development, 68

B

Ballia District
  literacy (2001), 72, 73
  literacy rate, 73
  female literacy, rate, 73
  initiatives, 73
Banks initiatives in micro-credit, 107, 129
Basic (foundation) education, 144
Bhagria (1992), 32
Bhandari (1974), 31
Bharathidasan University
  Tiruchirappalli course for BPO, 108
Bhatia (1982), 92
Bhatia (1996), 52, 96
Bijapur and Dakshina Kannada, 34
BPO
  expectation from employees, 109
  training, 108
Braham Prakash (1978), 32
Budget 2007-2008
  skills in demand, 103

C

Call centre industry training, 108
Campaign Approach, 56
Central Advisory Board of Education initiatives (1974), 39-40
Central Uttar Pradesh, 58
Central Board of Workers Education, 37
Chambers (1995), 120
Charcha Mandals, 49
Chaturvedi (1969), 25
Checklists to access the relevance of Adult education programme, 169
Choice of language, 93
Chugani (1987), 32
Civil Society Groups-support from, 36
Coaching Support to recipients of post-Matric Scholarships, 103
Colleges and Universities role played by, 96
Co-coordinating role, 164
Communication training Skills, 108-109
Composite Quality of life index, 119
'*Consolidating the past, Strengthening the Future*, (2004), 96
Constituencies for Knowledge dissemination, 99

Continuing education courses, 113
Coombs (1973), 117
Core faculty sanction, 167
Core work skills, 144
Corruption-eliminating, 139
Credit Access/Support initiatives for poor, 106, 129
Current Scenario, 150

D

Dave Committee on modalities of total literacy, 56
Decentralization, 69, 139
Department of Adult, Continuing and Extension Education, 97, 110
Status, 159
Nomenclature, 160
Structure, 160-61
Faculty, 162
Deen Dayal Upadhyay University Gorakhpur, works, 112
–courses
: Under Equivalency programme, 112
: Vocational, 113
: Continuing Education, 114
Desirable changes, 19
Development Projects, 95
Directorate of Literacy and Adult Education, 67, 95
Dixit (1975), 26
Documentation and dissemination of information, 165
Dreze and Sen (1995), 61
Drop out rates factors, 30-31
Dubashi (1983), 119

E

Eastern U.P., 58
study-limitations, 73-74
literacy-initiatives suggested, 79
NAEP, 71
T.L.C. campaign, 71, 77
Economic
Development and Literacy, 136
Performance and literacy, 119
Educational access, 120
Educational Programme, 18
Education and Health role in development, 61
Education (general) purpose, 117-18
E-Governance, 104
Elementry education system (India), 81
Eleventh Five Year Plan -Objectives, 97
Empowerments needs of poor, 137-38
Enrolment-spread, 81-82
Equivalency Programmes, 156
Ernakulum District –T.L.C, 51

Evaluation of Literacy and Adult Education Programme, 33
Extension
need for, 147
as third dimension, 148
Extension function of the institution of higher education, 44, 109
Extension Lectures, 95

F

Faculty/staff of Department of Adult, Continuing and Extension Education, 162
Farmers Functional Literacy Programme, 32
Female literacy rates, 65
low rates region-UP, 67, 69
Field Outreach focus areas, 153
Five Year Plans, 97
on literacy panels, 38-39
Formal education and training, 144
programme elements, 144
Functionality component of NAEP, 42
Functional
Science, 28
Literacy, 91
Funding Criteria and pattern of Assistance-UGC, 166

G

Gadgil (1945), 30
Gains from Literacy, 31
Gains in functionality-eastern UP, 76, 80
Gender-related development index (GDI), 61, 63
Gram Shikshan Muhim (1959), 37
Guidelines issued by UGC, 93-94

H

Health and education role in development, 61
Higher education expansion, 82
Historical Perspective, 35
Human Development
Report 2003-UP, 59-60, 63, 66
-accessment, 62
Meaning, 60
(HDI), 60, 61

I

IGNOU-role, 101-102
ILO initiative, 108
Implementation Committee on Continuing and Extension Education Dept. in University, 161
Imperial Chemical Industries-Employees Education, 36
Indian Education Commission Report on Night Schools (1982), 35

Indian University Association for Continuing education (IUACE), 88
Individual interest promotion programs, 156
Infrastructure (university) for placement growth, 101
Industrial Workers Panel for literacy, 39
Initiatives for literacy, 36
Instructor effectiveness training, 29
Interview Schedule for Various Functionaries in Adult Education programme, 175

J

Jacob (1990), 28
Jalaluddin (1980), 40-41, 119
Jana Shikshan Nilayam (JSN), 49
 activities, 49
 levels of literacy, 49
 failures causes, 50
J & K Adult education programme-review, 34
Jayagopal
 on Andragogy, 22
 on role of teacher, 24

K

Kaur (1992), 29
Kerala Adult Education, 29
Khan (1958), 30
Knowles assumptions (4) on learners life, 21
Kudesia (1975), 31

L

Language Choice, 93
Leadership and Human Resource Development, 155
Learning
 Process, 18, 21
 Concepts, 19
 Packages for illiterates, 29
Lifelong learning, 144
Liquidation of Illiteracy Committee, 36
Literacy, 17
 and Development, 119
 Conceptualization, 53
 role, 122
 Functionary Groups, 91
Literacy Campaign
 planning -consideration, 24
 failure-causes, 53
Literacy and Adult Education
 content, concern, 117
 role in socio-economic development, 32
 initiatives, 54
 shifting perspectives, 54
 insights, 55
Literate Society, 121
Literacy rate
 census 2001, 63
 gender gap scenario, 63
 urban-rural differential, 64
 SC-ST, 64

disparities, 65-66
Liveright and Haygood, 18
Local language based
documentation-subjects, 134

M

Mali (1974), 30
Management Sensitivity/Shift, 44-45
Mass Programmes of literacy, 40
Micro-Credit
demand, 107
programmes, 103
Ministry of Education NSS Scheme, 88
Mohan and Usha (1992), 34
Mother Tongue role in literacy, 26
research/views, 27
effects of using, 28
Motivation to acquire Literacy, 25
Motivational Strategies, 34
MPFL Tamil Nadu, 52

N

NABARD, 129
Credit initatives for poor, 129
Nagappa (1966), 30
Nagpur University
NAEP, 44
Bifurcation, 45
National Adult Education Programme (NAEP), 41
20 Point Programme, 90
reference, 74
role, 90
components, 42
benefits, 75-76
Eastern UP, 71
National Knowledge Commission, 83
recommendations on vocational education, 84
National Literacy Mission, 51, 123
on urban Literacy Project, 124
2007 on literacy differentials, 64
National Service Scheme (NSS), 88, 95
NGOs
training programme, 133
view on literacy programmes, 124
Night Schools, 35
Report on (1982), 35
Nodal Universities, 164
Roles, 165-67

O

Olson and Torrance, 17-18
on literacy campaigns, 24
(2001), 53, 121
Organization and Conduct of Adult Education Agencies, -Kerala, 29

P

Panchayati Raj Institutions
women participation, 120
Planning Commissions Panel
for literacy, 39
Planning and Government
initiatives, 67
Policy Frame on Developments
of Higher Education (1977),
94
Poor People
attitude to literacy/scenario,
128
Access to market
infrastructure, 129
Conditions of stages, 136
Poverty, 128
pockets
watch indicators, 132-33
Post Literacy and Continuing
Education, 49
Post-Independence Phase, 35-36
1947-1977, 36
Post 1978 Phase, 40
Poverty Watch indicator, 132-33
Profiling of the poor in rural
areas, 131-32
Pro-poor research issues, 141

Q

Quality of life
Improvement Program, 156
Index, 119

R

Radio learning, 122
Rajan (1992), 52
Ramadin (1990), 29
Rashid (1966), 25
Reading/Writing, 20
Recognition of commitment to
teach, 98-99
Reddy (1990), 29
Resource Support Programme,
156
Retail Credit Outlets, 130
Retention of literacy skills, 30
factors affecting, 30-31
Right to Information /
Monitoring of Development
Programmes of Poor, 131
Rural poverty poor, 126
factors inducing, 126
access to developmental
rights, 127
Rural Functional Literacy
Project, 43
North Arcot District (TN),
32

S

Sachchidananda
(1992) on Samu, 52
et al (1991), 122
Saints-literature of, 28
Saksharata Muzaffarpur
Programme, 52
Saldhana etal (1991), 44

SC-ST literacy rate 2001, 64
Schools System –enrolment expansion, 81-82
Self Employment Initiatives, 103
Self Help Groups (SHG), 129
  initiatives, 107
Sensitization of the academic community, 86-87
Service Sector-Manpower needs, 104
Sharma (1990), 32
Shramik Vidyapeeths role, impact, 32-33
SIDBI initiatives, 130
Singh (1980), 87-88
Sixth Five Year Plan, 41
Skill areas for training, 106
Slum Settings
  literacy in, 123
  areas in, 125
Social education programme
  training centres, 37
  impact, 31
  role, 37
Social and Citizenship Role Awareness Programs, 156
Social literacy, 121
Social Capital Formation Processes, 140
Socio-cultural perspectives, 94
Southern U.P., 58
Special Economic Zones (SEZs) initiative, 102
Srivastava
  (1969), 25
  (1980), 28
State Resource Centers 67, 95
  role, tasks, 68
Story method of presentation, 30
Strategies adopted to spread literacy, 36
Survival needs of the poor, 136
Swaranjayanti
  Gram Swarozgar Yojana, 103
  Shahari Rozgar Yojana, 103

T

Talukdar (1975), 33
Tantray (1990), 34
Teaching, Training and Research Department, 157-58
Teachers role, 24
Technical Education, 33
Technical Resource Support, 95
Tenth Five Year Plan
  Target Groups, 153
  UGC guidelines, 147
  Thrusts, 151-52
Thakre (1991), 44-45
Third Dimension, 148
Total literacy campaign (TLC)
  Bijapur and Dakshina Kannada, 34
  Ernakulum
    District, 51
  Features, 51
  Eastern UP, 71, 77
    test/scores, 78-79
    sample research, 72, 77
    constraints, 78

Training Areas required in universities, 105
Triebel (2001), 122

U

UGC
  Guidelines on Adult, Continuing and Extension, Education, 147
  -1979, 93
  initiatives, 43
  programs and activities suggested 88, 174
Universities
  India (nos), 81
  role, 81
  assessment, 85
  issues being examined, 87
  activities undertaken by, 89
  activities-suggested for, 135-136
  role played, 96
  issues, questions, 99-100
  changes post Tenth FYP, 150
University Dept. on Adult Education, 38
University of Gorakhpur
  size of the program, 177
UP
  socio- economic development, 57
  divisions, 57
    western, central, eastern, southern regions, 57-58
  population, 58-59
  human development report, 2003, 59, 66
  literacy and adult education, 63
  literacy rate, 64
  gender gaps, 65
  urban-rural differentials, 65
  low female literacy, 67

V

Veeraraghavan (1980), 86
Verma (2002), 125
Vocational Education Mission, 86
Vocational and Technical Education, 33
Vocational Career Oriented Courses/Programs, 155

W

Wardha District (Maharashtra) evaluation, 33
Well-being and developmental needs of poor, 137
Western UP, 57
Women Learners, 122

Z

Zila Saksharata Samitis (ZSSs), 52, 55